BRAVOMAN

SUPER-UNEQUALED HERO OF EXCELLENCE!

™

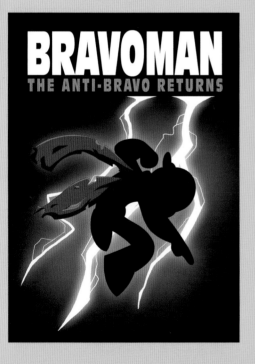

FOREWORD

Everyone loves Bravoman, especially me! All I did as a kid was play *Bravoman* on the TurboGrafx-16, pushing my way through level after level of platforming madness, trying desperately to defeat the evil Dr. Bomb and his Robot Corps. I had Bravoman posters in my bedroom, dressed as Bravoman every Halloween, and even named the family dog Bravo!

That's all lies, of course. I'd never heard of *Bravoman* before getting the assignment to reimagine the game as a webcomic. Indeed, I have never even touched a TurboGrafx-16 in my life. But even so, as I researched this obscure vintage video game, I found plenty of great nuggets to use as a foundation upon which to build a nearly all-new property.

There is certainly something intriguing about Bravoman and his universe. There's a level of wackiness to it that few properties can match. Half of that is intentional, as *Bravoman* was originally meant to be a sort of parody of both 1980s video games and Japanese superheroes. The other half comes, I think, from the game's transition from Japan to North America. The game is full of Engrishy translations, Japanese items like rice balls and lottery wheels, and enemies covering everything from floating robot heads to living totem poles. Top it all off with a main character whose super powers include ultra-stretchy limbs, plus the ability to turn into a submarine for some reason...

Even today, after us Westerners have had plenty of exposure to Japanese anime and games, it all seems pretty off-the-wall. I can't imagine what it must have been like to a kid picking this up in 1990.

Our new version of *Bravoman* might actually be just as weird and wacky, though in different ways. I hope you enjoy the fourth-wall-breaking, meta-humor-infused world that Dax and I have come up with. Welcome to *Bravoman: Super-Unequaled Hero of Excellence!*

MATT MOYLAN
WRITER, BRAVOMAN

A BRIEF HISTORY OF BRAVOMAN & NAMCO

Until very recently, Bravoman only ever had the one video game 25 years ago. But someone at Namco Bandai must really like the little superhero, as he has popped up in several places over the years.

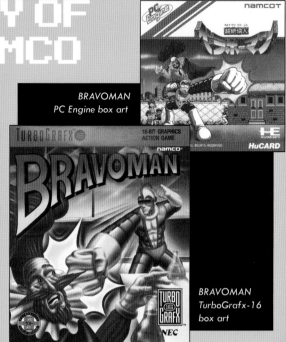

BRAVOMAN PC Engine box art

BRAVOMAN TurboGrafx-16 box art

The original *Bravoman* was an arcade game released in Japan in 1988. It's basically a side-scrolling beat-em-up where you go around using your stretchy limbs to smash robots, ninjas, monsters, etc. There are also a bunch of underwater levels where Bravoman transforms into a submarine and shoots torpedoes (random!). We never saw the arcade version here, but in 1990 the game was ported to the PC Engine game console, which North Americans know as the TurboGrafx-16. This ended the only official English console-based adventure for Bravoman, but back in Japan there's a little more to the story.

SPIN-OFFS & CAMEOS

1990 saw the release of another Namco arcade game – a *Bravoman* spin-off titled *PISTOL DAIMYO NO BOKEN*. Originally a boss character in *Bravoman*, Pistol Daimyo is a Japanese feudal lord with a pistol strapped to his head, who can fly by waving the hand-fans he holds with his feet. The game is a side-scrolling shooter where you blast away at frogs, birds, ninjas, and living sandals. Also, if you die, Pistol Daimyo does a little fan dance... naked. I think I can see why this game remained Japan-exclusive.

PISTOL DAIMYO NO BOKEN arcade game

BRAVOMAN on the PC Engine

Beyond that, Bravoman hasn't seen any more spin-offs, but he HAS had plenty of cameos! Probably the best-known of these is in the 2005 Japan-only action/tactical RPG *NAMCO X CAPCOM*, where Bravoman is teamed up with Wonder Momo (another old-school Namco character that has recently been rejuvenated with a ShiftyLook

(CONTINUED NEXT PAGE)

webcomic!). Other *Bravoman* characters also appear throughout the game, such as Waya Hime, Anti-Bravoman, Benjamin, Pistol Daimyo, and Dr. Bomb. It's notable that, in this game, ninja princess Waya Hime gets to team up with Taki, the *SOULCALIBUR* series' resident ninja babe. Taki had previously been given a Waya Hime alternate costume in 2002's *SOULCALIBUR II*.

More Bravoman cameos can be found in the arcade/SEGA Genesis game *MARVEL LAND* (1989), *NAMCO SUPER WARS* (2002) - an RPG for Bandai's Wonderswan handheld - and *NAMCO CHRONICLE*, a 2009 mobile phone RPG. Dr. Bomb makes a small cameo in *DIGITAL DEVIL STORY: MEGAMI TENSEI II* (2002), from back when Namco acted as the publisher for the then-fledgling game developer Atlus. Most recently, Bravoman appeared in *PRO BASEBALL FAMISTA 2011*, a Nintendo 3DS baseball game which features a special team made up entirely of Namco Bandai characters.

PRO BASEBALL FAMISTA 2011 promo art

MODERN REVIVAL

But as far as North America knew, after the original TurboGrafx-16 game, Bravoman was forever forgotten... that is, until he was resurrected as an original webcomic by ShiftyLook! As of this book's release, the webcomic is 250+ strips strong and still going. ShiftyLook has even spun *Bravoman* off into a series of animated web cartoons. The first season of these animated shorts features an all-star voice cast, including Rob Paulsen (*TMNT*, *Animaniacs*), Dee Bradley Baker (*American Dad!*), Romi Dames (*Winx Club*) and Jennifer Hale (*Mass Effect*). ShiftyLook has also produced *Bravoman: Binja Bash!*, a mobile game available on the iOS and Android platforms. The game is an on-rails 2D platformer where Bravoman and other characters fight their way through Dr. Bomb's endless army of robot ninjas.

BRAVOMAN animated web cartoon

INSPIRATION FROM MASAYA NAKAMURA

A lot of superheroes have a mild-mannered secret identity. Superman is reporter Clark Kent, Spider-Man is photographer Peter Parker. For Bravoman that role is Salaryman, an average Japanese business man. While he barely appears in the game, and in the webcomic we've only shown him briefly in the first strip, I think Salaryman is a big part of why Bravoman is given so many video game cameos. That's because Salaryman is actually a caricature of Masaya Nakamura – the founder of Namco Bandai.

Nakamura started the company in 1955 as Nakamura Manufacturing Ltd., to produce children's rides. The company name would later be changed to Nakamura Manufacturing Co., and in 1971 was shortened to just Namco. Namco first got into the video game business in 1974 when Nakamura purchased the struggling Japanese division of Atari, folding it into his own company. During the late '70s and early '80s, Namco started creating its own games with *GEE BEE*, *GALAXIAN*, *PAC-MAN*, *DIG DUG*, *XEVIOUS*, and one day... *Bravoman*! In 2005, Namco merged with toy and video game giant Bandai to become Namco Bandai Games Inc.

Nakamura is now considered one of the founding fathers of the video game industry, and has been recognized several times for it. In 2007 he was presented with The Order of the Rising Sun (Gold Rays with Rosette), one of Japan's highest honors, for his contributions to Japanese industry. In 2010 Nakamura was inducted into the International Video Game Hall of Fame alongside Namco Bandai's most recognizable character: Pac-Man.

Even now as a man in his 80s, Nakamura is still looking to the future. After receiving the Order of the Rising Sun, he remarked, "I express my sincere appreciation and gratitude for all people who supported me. In order to grow and prosper in the rapidly changing Contents industry, a flexible way of thinking and actions becomes essential. I would like to entrust our future to the younger generations and expect them to succeed."

Salaryman

BRAVOMAN arcade game promo poster

PLAY BRAVOMAN !

Bringing it all back to where it started, if you want to play *Bravoman* for yourself, you actually can! No, you don't have to go scouring flea markets for a TurboGrafx-16... the original *Bravoman* is available as a downloadable game on the Nintendo Wii Virtual Console. Be warned... it's really hard! But give it a shot if you're in the mood for some good old 1980s video game wackiness!

COMMENTS

MATT: Our adventure begins! This is pretty much the same as the character's origin in the original Japanese game. It's so random and brief! Bravoman's origin is probably less important than that of the average superhero, and we've rarely called back to it in future strips. Actually, the only time we have really referenced it is when giving origin strips to other characters.

DAX: And here we go! This was actually the third strip we finished, but the first that was created once we had been green-lit by ShiftyLook. Exciting times!

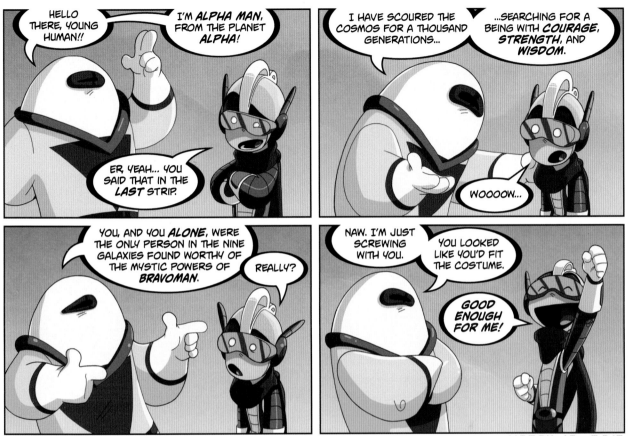

#002: ALPHA TALE

MARCH 10, 2012

COMMENTS

MATT: I'm surprised at the number of exclamation points Alpha has in this early strip. These days, I consciously try to avoid exclamation points for him, so he always seems calm and collected. Nothing phases Alpha Man. Well... almost nothing.

DAX: I remember this is when I started to get a feel for Bravo's personality and how we could push his expression dramatically from panel to panel. Always fun to be able to do as an artist.

ROUGH LAYOUT

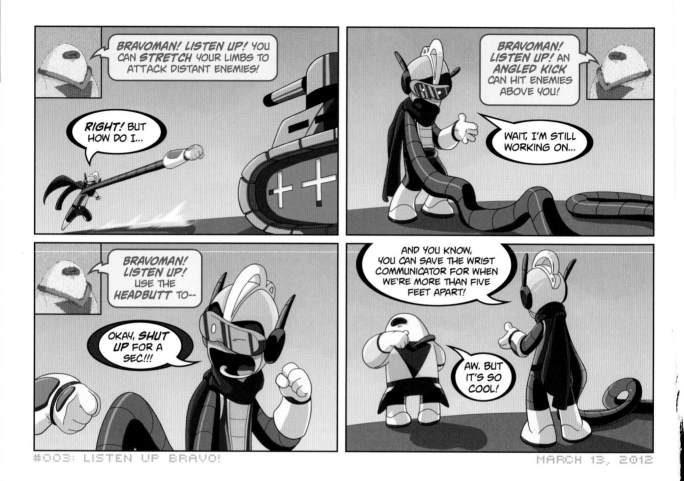

#003: LISTEN UP BRAVO!

MARCH 13, 2012

COMMENTS

MATT: I HATE those games that won't stop bothering you with incessant help messages. I'd rather be thrown into a game world and figure stuff out on my own. This strip was animated as one of the teaser/test animations for the *Bravoman* animated web series.

DAX: Ah yes, the stretchy limbs! We spent a large chunk of the early part of the series making Bravo a hero struggling to get ahold of his new powers. Always fun to play with this stuff visually.

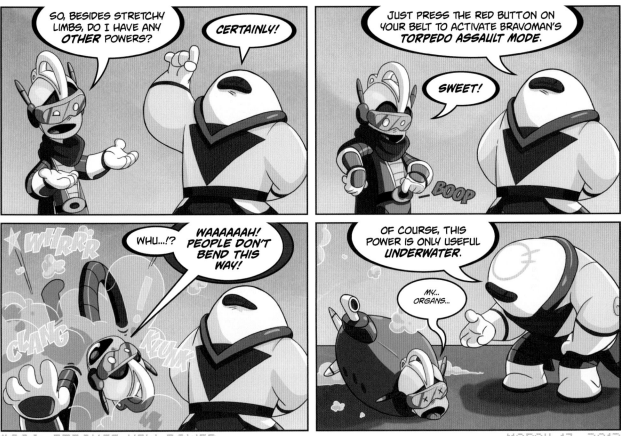

#004: STRANGE NEW POWER

MARCH 17, 2012

COMMENTS

MATT: This was actually the very first strip created as part of the initial *Bravoman* pitch package Dax and I put together for ShiftyLook. You've come a long way, boys! Originally I had intended for all of Bravoman's new powers to be controlled by pressing the same button in a different way. It's still an idea I might pick up later in an alternate way.

DAX: This is the first strip I penciled and colored, and if you flip closer to the end of this book, you can see how far the series has come artistically. I used to cringe when I saw these old strips, but now I think it shows history and adds some charm to the series. Notice the UDON symbol I thought would be cute on Alpha's head. I decided to do away with it after this one and only appearance.

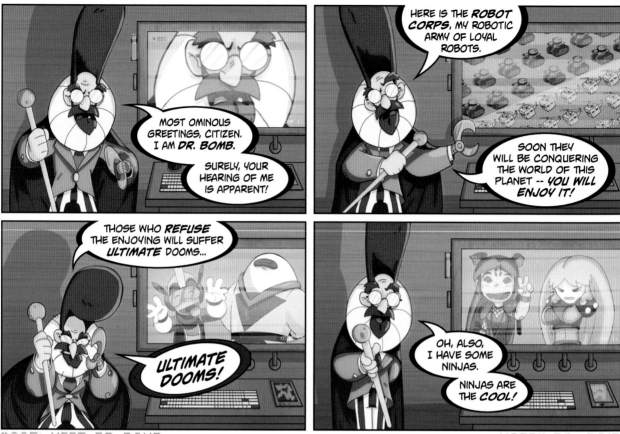

COMMENTS

MATT: Dr. Bomb's speech is one of the clearest callbacks to the original *Bravoman* game. The North American release of the game had a hilariously bad English translation, with such great Engrish lines as "I am Japanese telephone box." and "Who is rising against me?" It's actually tough to write dialog that is badly spoken but still understandable.

DAX: Introducing DR. BOMB! I spent a long time on this one… At the time, he was the only character that didn't fit the shape language of the rest of the cast. (Waya, Benjamin, Bravo, etc. are all roughly the same height and shape.)

#006: ANTI-BRAVO RISES

MARCH 24, 2012

COMMENTS

MATT: Anti-Bravoman is one of my favorite characters. I feel bad about how mean we are to him, but at the same time... that's the whole point! He wants so bad to be a dark and sinister character, but can't help letting his awkward nerd side come out.

DAX: Anti-Bravo! Or **A.B.** as he is now called, instantly became the most popular character in the series. Everyone always seems to connect with this wannabe anti-hero. This is also the first appearance of the pigeon, who a friend of mine called "cute." So moving forward, every time I drew A.B., the pigeon wasn't too far behind, and grew into a full-fledged character almost 100 strips later!

#007: PRE-EMPTED

MARCH 27, 2012

COMMENTS

MATT: Waya Hime is probably Anti-Bravoman's closest competitor in the running for the series' most popular character. I love both her endless enthusiasm towards her goals, and her unique pink/green/blue color scheme. She really stands out visually, which is saying something with our cast of literally colorful characters.

DAX: Waya Hime! Drawing Waya has always been fun for me, as I get to explore the cute *kawaii* angle as well as an angry, ferocious and action-packed ninja side of things.

#008: POINTY PRINCESS

MARCH 31, 2012

COMMENTS

MATT: I think this strip perfectly encapsulates Waya's character. She is both in love with and assigned to kill Bravoman. What's unique about Waya is that she is not at all conflicted over this contradiction. She's able to compartmentalize both goals, and pursues each of them with all of her heart.

DAX: This was the first script where I saw how Waya's character was going to go. Love vs. Training... a common trend in the *Bravoman* universe. I feel it's a big part of what gives the series its carefree, fun and easy-to-read vibe.

ROUGH LAYOUT

APRIL 03, 2012

COMMENTS

MATT: Alpha's role as a passive instigator starts to set in here. He's always on Bravoman's side, but his actions (or inaction) tend to get Bravo into trouble.

DAX: Are those lips or is that his eye? The color of his visor probably doesn't help answer this question, nor does the fact that we had him mysteriously take a bite of his sandwich off-panel. But still, it has been one of those fun things that fans have talked about for quite some time now. We really need to do a strip that sets the record straight, Matt. :P

ROUGH LAYOUT

#010: THE PRINCESS PRIDE   APRIL 07, 2012

COMMENTS

MATT: We used this same joke in the animated series, and it's one of the rare cases where people thought we were too mean to a character. (Though really, Anti-Bravoman gets kicked around much worse than this, heh.) Luckily, Waya seems to have gotten over the insult completely by her next appearance. Also, *reverse tsundere* was the best term I could come up with at the time. I would later learn that *yandere* is a much better term to specifically describe Waya's personality. Go ahead, Google that too.

DAX: He was under duress, I don't think he actually meant it...

ROUGH LAYOUT

COMMENTS

MATT: The blueprint strips were something I started doing to help Dax get ahead on strip production. I drew the blueprint portion while Dax only needed to create the single inset panels. It's been fun getting to occasionally contribute artwork to the series. The *Bravoman* franchise's love affair with net launchers also begins here.

DAX: I've always loved these. I think Matt should do more, what do you think?

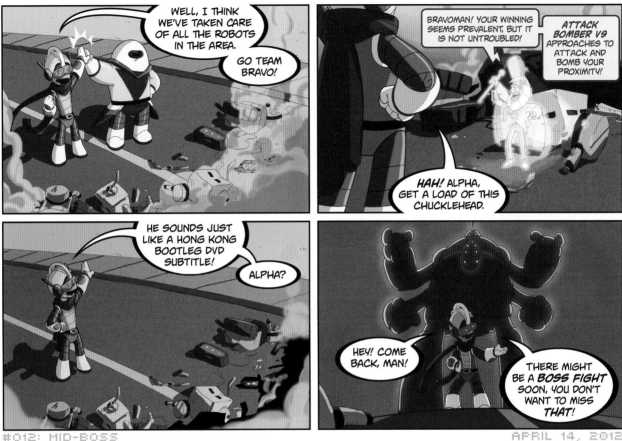

#012: MID-BOSS

COMMENTS

MATT: The mini hologram is one of the rare times that Bravoman has actually encountered Dr. Bomb in the series, which is kind of odd considering he is our chief villain.

DAX: This was the first time I got to draw Attack Bomber V9 since the poster art! Obviously a lot of fun was had playing with the scale in panel four.

ROUGH LAYOUT

#013: PRODUCT PLACEMENT

COMMENTS

MATT: One of my favorite early strips, I still love how well the pacing of this gag worked out. This is also our first hint that Bravoman is self-aware of his own media and merchandising history (both the real and fictional parts).

DAX: Lots of stuff going on here, as it was the first action mini arc of the series. I always enjoy these arcs, as they let me play with some fun angles and posing!

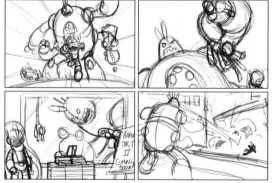

ROUGH LAYOUT

COMMENTS

MATT: This is the first time that Bravoman straight up breaks the fourth wall to defeat an enemy, and it really sets the standard for the ongoing tone of the series. My general philosophy is that while many of the characters are self-aware of their fictional existence and the tropes that come with it, Bravoman is the only one who can use that knowledge to manipulate events.

DAX: Definitely getting to pay homage to my love of anime here. Whenever I draw action stuff, it is heavily influenced by it. You will notice this more in later strips.

ROUGH LAYOUT

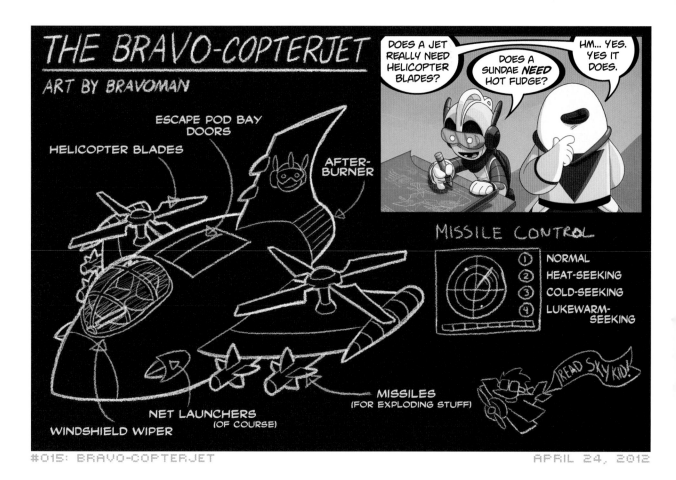

COMMENTS

MATT: Went through a lot of names for this one; helijet, hoverplane, jetcopter... Honestly, I think I chose **copterjet** because it was the most awkward. The little doodle in the bottom-right corner is a reference to *Sky Kid*, the second webcomic series that UDON produced as part of the initial ShiftyLook website launch.

DAX: I want one.

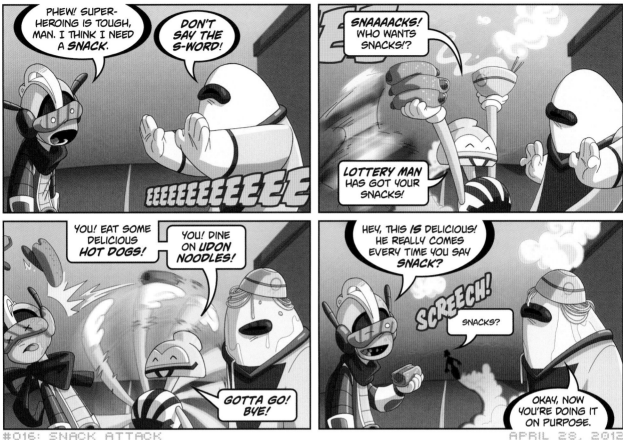

#016: SNACK ATTACK

APRIL 28, 2012

COMMENTS

MATT: Lottery Man is Bravoman's second sidekick from the original game, in which he is a helper who provides Bravoman with food that replenishes his energy meter. In our version, Lottery Man is an imperfectly functioning food service robot who is obsessed with snacks. He's also the only character who is able to get under Alpha's skin. Every character needs to be taken down a peg once in a while. *laughs*

DAX: Lottery Man! SNACKS!!! I enjoyed drawing Alpha deadpanning the camera in this one because it's the first time he hasn't been all too impressed with someone or something in the series. Generally he is super positive and upbeat. Not with Lottery Man, though. *laughs*

ROUGH LAYOUT

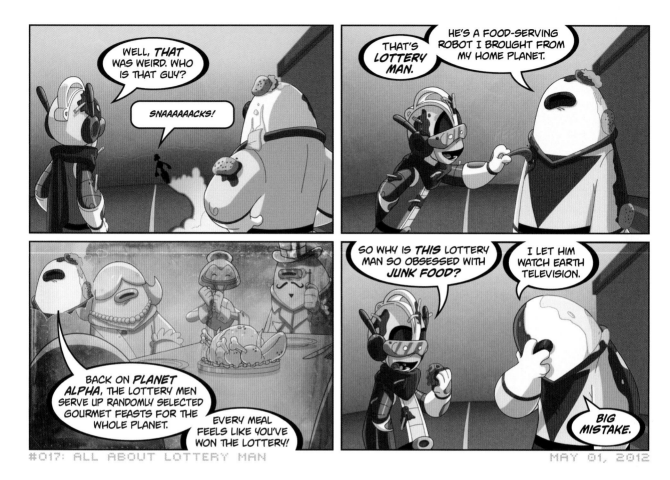

COMMENTS

MATT: I loved the designs Dax came up with for the random Alphans in the flashback so much that they would eventually return as full-fledged characters. You never know when a one-off gag will provide continuity fodder later on.

DAX: Here is another example of something I now look at as #charm and #history. Awww yes, good times. You never stop getting better, kids; remember that and keep drawing!

ROUGH LAYOUT

#013: FANCY ANGLES

MAY 05, 2012

COMMENTS

MATT: The angle in panel one was something Dax originally wanted to do in Waya Hime's first appearance, but I asked him to change it so we get a clearer view of Waya Hime right away. Glad he got to reuse it here. Also, the speech-impaired cyborg Benjamin joins our cast of baddies!

DAX: I've always liked how the angles in this one turned out. Lots of foreshortening, and it took me some time to get it right but I feel for the most part that it was successful.

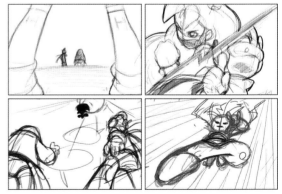

ROUGH LAYOUT

#019: HIGHER POWER

MAY 08, 2012

COMMENTS

MATT: Whoa, man! Mentioning that your meta elements are meta? That's ULTRA META.

DAX: Ah yes, my first official shout-out in the series! *laughs* That's right Bravo, preach brother!

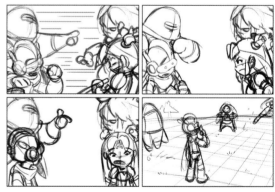

ROUGH LAYOUT

COMMENTS

MATT: The script asked Dax to design a guitar-sword for Benjamin. It was Dax's idea that a keytar-sword would be more unique and also fit better with Benjamin's big hair, 1980s metal vibe. Good call, partner!

DAX: Love that sword... but it's a lot of lines to draw...

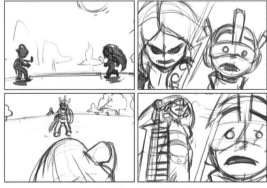

ROUGH LAYOUT

#021: UNIVERSAL HUMOR

COMMENTS

MATT: I think the **stupid punny universe** part is me berating my own cheesy joke. Don't think something is funny enough? Comment on how unfunny it is!

DAX: Why wouldn't a banjo drop from the sky?! #SoBravo

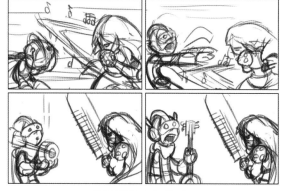

ROUGH LAYOUT

#022: WE CAN'T HEAR YOU

MAY 19, 2012

COMMENTS

MATT: So, not only do the characters understand that they're fictional, they also know what specific medium they exist in. AND they care about quality entertainment; that's always appreciated.

DAX: The wrist communicator's first appearance. Well, the first time you get to see what the viewscreen looks like anyway. :P

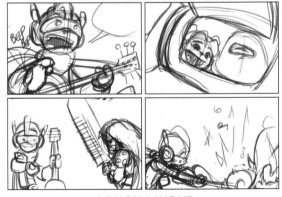

ROUGH LAYOUT

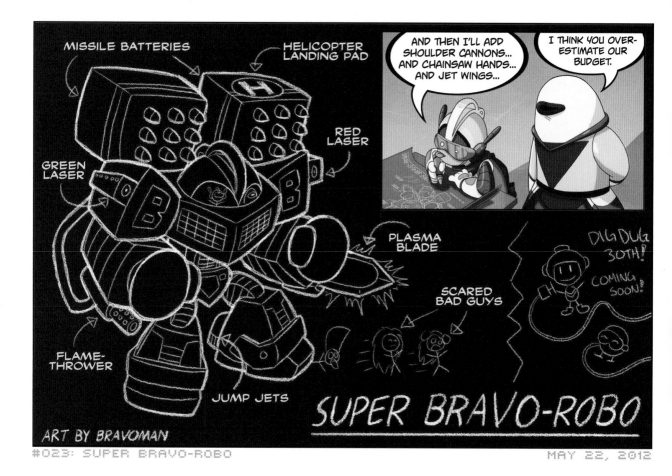

COMMENTS

MATT: Super-deformed robots are what I'm most known for drawing, so I guess this one was inevitable. The green laser is a reference to *Robot Jox,* the best live action fighting robots movie EVER (take THAT *Pacific Rim*).

DAX: WANT.

#024: HIDDEN ALLY   MAY 26, 2012

COMMENTS

MATT: I like that there's a little story happening with the characters on the ground without any words. Need to try something like this out again sometime.

DAX: Getting to draw Waya and Benjamin in this one was my favorite part. Something about dragging a body out of the scene is just funny to me… poor Benjamin.

ROUGH LAYOUT

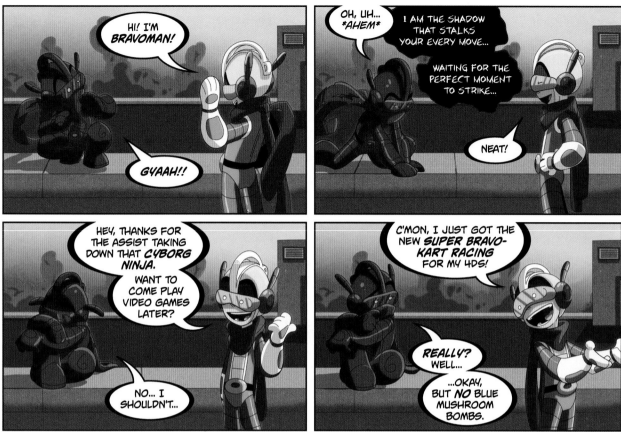

#025: BRAVO BUDDIES   MAY 29, 2012

COMMENTS

MATT: The first direct meeting of Bravoman and Anti-Bravoman! Poor A.B., this will not end well.

DAX: I've always wanted these two to be friends. But I like how Matt is keeping it at bay for the sake of the story. It adds tension nicely! Maybe someday!

ROUGH LAYOUT

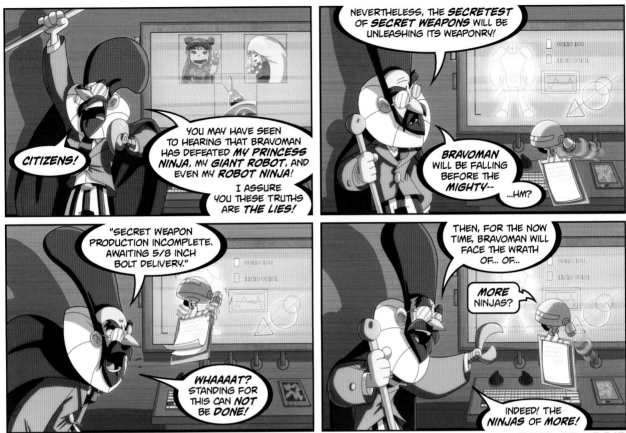

COMMENTS

MATT: I came up with Hoverbot so that Dr. Bomb would have someone to interact with if needed when doing his ranting. Hoverbot is inspired by Megatron's drone from the show *Beast Machines* (probably the best thing to come from that show!).

DAX: It's funny, I realized as I was cleaning this one up that Dr. Bomb is basically a caricature of my father. *laughs* You're famous, Pops!

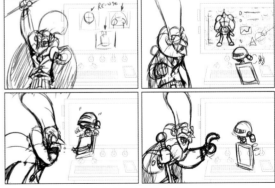

ROUGH LAYOUT

#027: ROOFTOP RAMBLINGS

COMMENTS

MATT: It'd take us a bit before we used the Binjas more often, but these guys are basically our disposable foot soldiers. Obviously they are based on Benjamin's design; he is essentially their unit leader. The original idea was that they came in two colors and that there were 100 of them in total.

This is also the strip where Josh Perez joined Team Bravo as our colorist. Previously Dax had handled full art chores, but we were moving from twice a week to three times, and so Dax needed more time to focus on line art. Josh has turned out to be a great addition, and now we couldn't do the strips without him!

DAX: Not sure we have seen this since, but Binjas transform from egg-like cocoons. Now make the transforming noise for me while you read the strip. *cheee choo chhooo choo chuu cheeeech*

#028: BRAVO-WHO?!

JUNE 09, 2012

COMMENTS

MATT: Since the Binjas are just mindless robots and based on Benjamin, Bravo Woman was the first real character that Dax and I created from scratch. The idea is so obvious that she pretty much willed herself into existence. Still, I think we fleshed her out later into a fun character.

DAX: Bravo WOMAN!!! She has changed so much from her original design... #charm #history

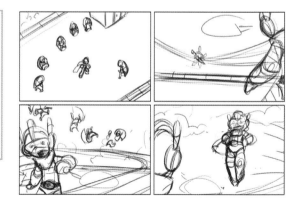

ROUGH LAYOUT

THE SUPER SECRET ORIGIN OF BRAVO WOMAN!

DAX AND MATT WERE JUST TWO ORDINARY WEBCOMIC CREATORS, UNTIL...

EVERYBODY LOVES *BRAVOMAN!* YOU SHOULD MAKE A *GIRL* VERSION OF HIM!

WELL THAT'S... REDUNDANT.

OUR HEROES ARE ENTRUSTED WITH *A WRITING QUILL, A DRAWING PENCIL,* AND *A STACK OF CASH.*

I'M CONVINCED!

ME TOO!

AS MYSTIC POWERS ARE UNLEASHED...

...A NEW HEROINE IS BORN!

BRAVO WOMAN

GIRL HERO OF MAXIMUM JUSTICE

BEING DERIVATIVE HAS NEVER LOOKED SO *BUTT-KICKINGLY* GOOD!

#029: THE ORIGIN OF BRAVO WOMAN   JUNE 12, 2012

COMMENTS

MATT: Our first of many revisitings of the origin strip format. And again we get another non-origin, really. Later on we gave Bravo Woman more background, but you'll have to wait until Vol. 2 for that. Oh, props to Dax as well for his likenesses of the two of us! Not the last time we'll show up...

DAX: ShiftyLook Editor in Chief Rob Pereyda makes his first appearance! You can find him dotted throughout the series, and in the cartoon as well.

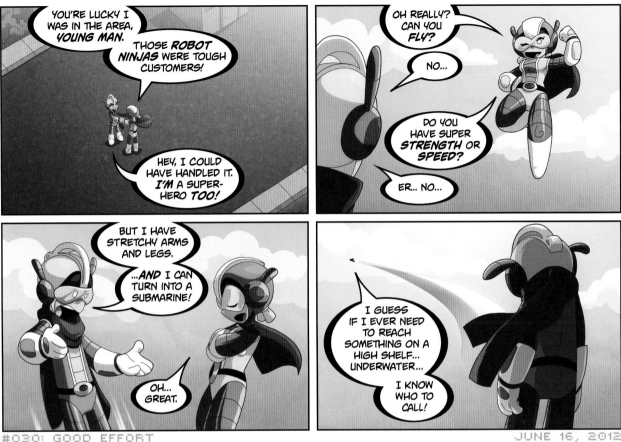

#030: GOOD EFFORT

JUNE 16, 2012

COMMENTS

MATT: Bravo Woman is what some people call a *flying brick*, which is any character whose powers are roughly the same as those of Superman (mainly super strength and flight).

DAX: Keep your head up, Bravo…

ROUGH LAYOUT

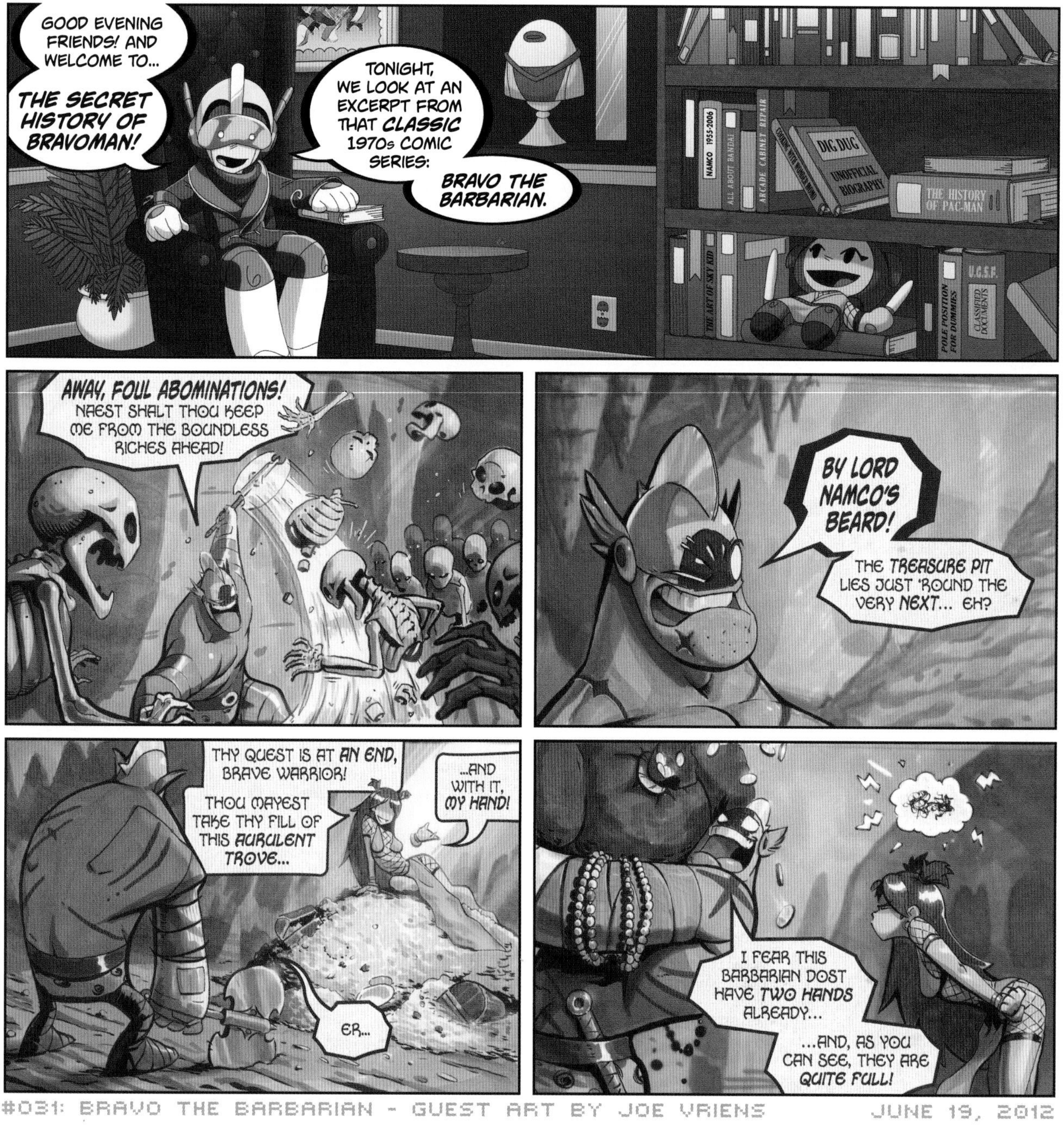
GOOD EVENING FRIENDS! AND WELCOME TO...
THE SECRET HISTORY OF BRAVOMAN!
TONIGHT, WE LOOK AT AN EXCERPT FROM THAT CLASSIC 1970s COMIC SERIES:
BRAVO THE BARBARIAN.
DIG DUG UNOFFICIAL BIOGRAPHY
THE HISTORY OF PAC-MAN
NAMCO 1955-2006
ALL ABOUT BANDAI
ARCADE CABINET REPAIR
THE ART OF SKY KID
POLE POSITION FOR DUMMIES
U.G.S.F. CLASSIFIED DOCUMENTS
AWAY, FOUL ABOMINATIONS! NAEST SHALT THOU KEEP ME FROM THE BOUNDLESS RICHES AHEAD!
BY LORD NAMCO'S BEARD!
THE TREASURE PIT LIES JUST 'ROUND THE VERY NEXT... EH?
THY QUEST IS AT AN END, BRAVE WARRIOR!
THOU MAYEST TAKE THY FILL OF THIS AURULENT TROVE...
...AND WITH IT, MY HAND!
ER...
I FEAR THIS BARBARIAN DOST HAVE TWO HANDS ALREADY...
...AND, AS YOU CAN SEE, THEY ARE QUITE FULL!

#031: BRAVO THE BARBARIAN - GUEST ART BY JOE VRIENS JUNE 19, 2012

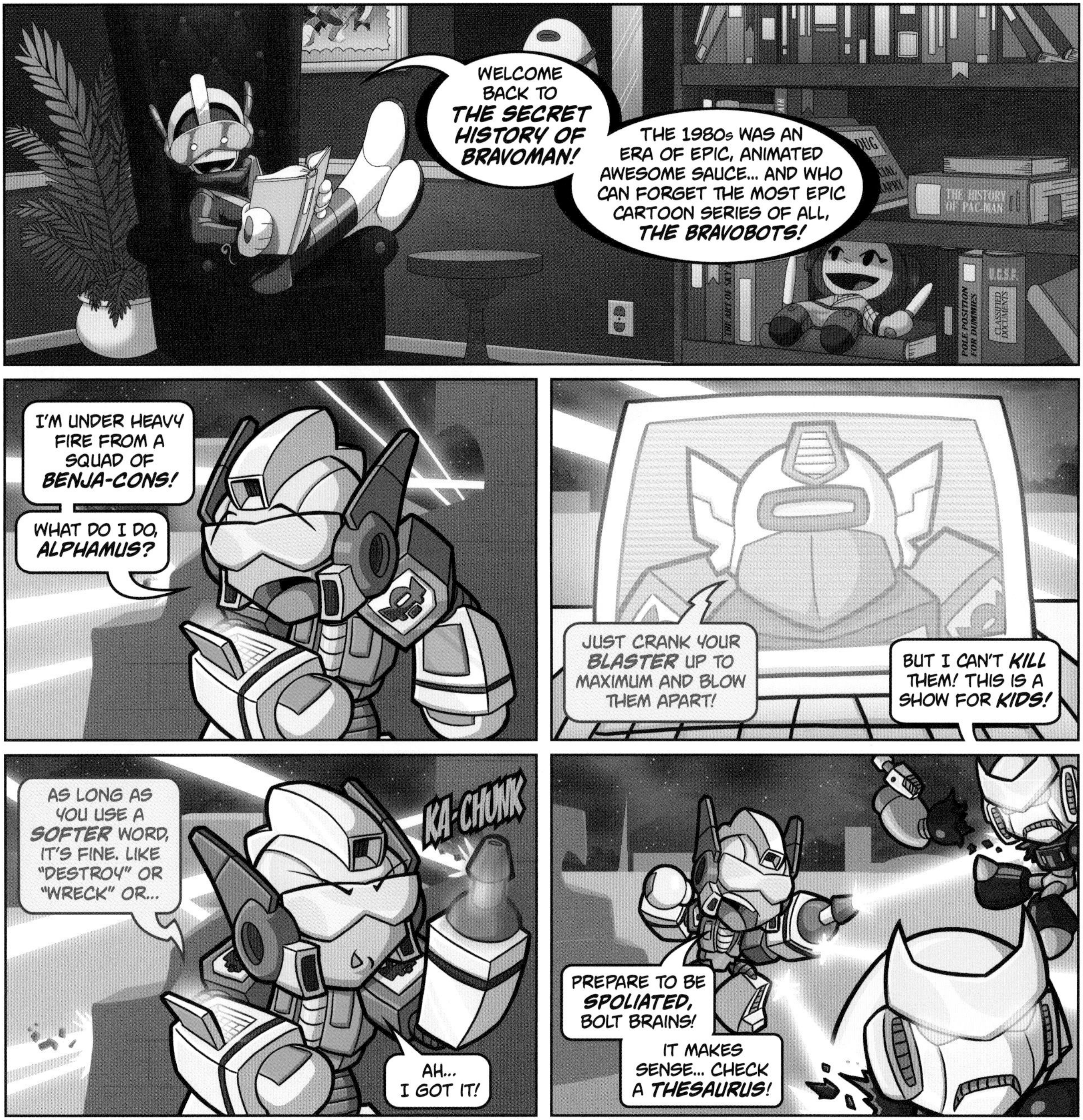
WELCOME BACK TO THE SECRET HISTORY OF BRAVOMAN!
THE 1980s WAS AN ERA OF EPIC, ANIMATED AWESOME SAUCE... AND WHO CAN FORGET THE MOST EPIC CARTOON SERIES OF ALL, THE BRAVOBOTS!
THE HISTORY OF PAC-MAN
U.G.S.F.
POLE POSITION FOR DUMMIES
CLASSIFIED DOCUMENTS
I'M UNDER HEAVY FIRE FROM A SQUAD OF BENJA-CONS!
WHAT DO I DO, ALPHAMUS?
JUST CRANK YOUR BLASTER UP TO MAXIMUM AND BLOW THEM APART!
BUT I CAN'T KILL THEM! THIS IS A SHOW FOR KIDS!
AS LONG AS YOU USE A SOFTER WORD, IT'S FINE. LIKE "DESTROY" OR "WRECK" OR...
KA-CHUNK
AH... I GOT IT!
PREPARE TO BE SPOLIATED, BOLT BRAINS!
IT MAKES SENSE... CHECK A THESAURUS!

#032: BRAVOBOTS - GUEST ART BY MATT MOYLAN JUNE 23, 2012

#033: BRAVO-CHAN - GUEST ART BY ROB "ROBAATO" PORTER   JUNE 26, 2012

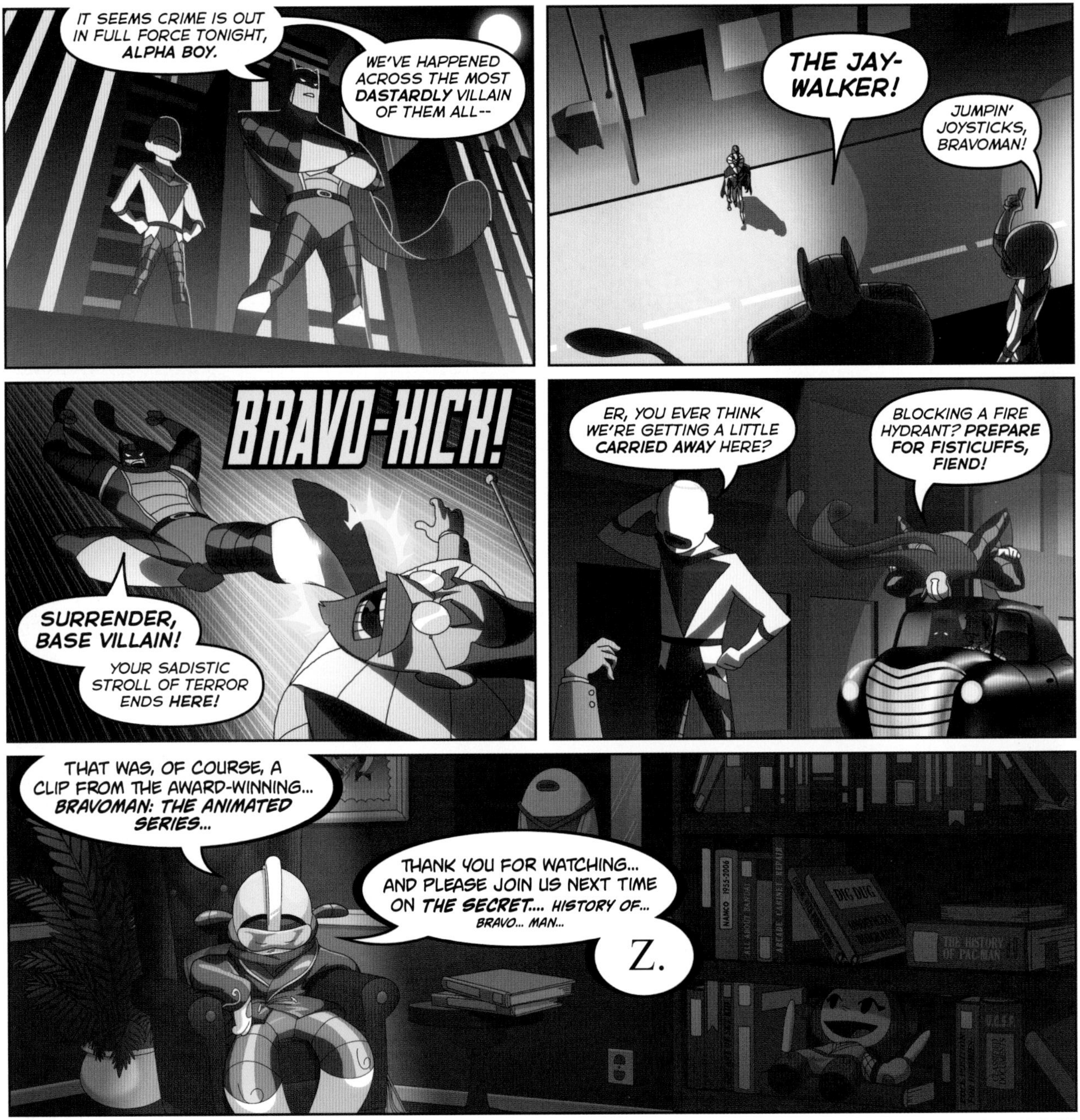
IT SEEMS CRIME IS OUT IN FULL FORCE TONIGHT, ALPHA BOY.
WE'VE HAPPENED ACROSS THE MOST DASTARDLY VILLAIN OF THEM ALL--
THE JAY-WALKER!
JUMPIN' JOYSTICKS, BRAVOMAN!
BRAVO-KICK!
SURRENDER, BASE VILLAIN!
YOUR SADISTIC STROLL OF TERROR ENDS HERE!
ER, YOU EVER THINK WE'RE GETTING A LITTLE CARRIED AWAY HERE?
BLOCKING A FIRE HYDRANT? PREPARE FOR FISTICUFFS, FIEND!
THAT WAS, OF COURSE, A CLIP FROM THE AWARD-WINNING... BRAVOMAN: THE ANIMATED SERIES...
THANK YOU FOR WATCHING... AND PLEASE JOIN US NEXT TIME ON THE SECRET.... HISTORY OF... BRAVO... MAN...
Z.

#034: BRAVOMAN & ALPHA BOY - GUEST ART BY JEFFREY CRUZ JUNE 30, 2012

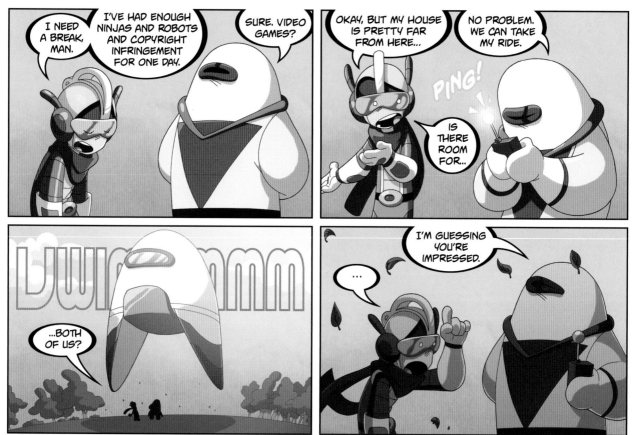

#035: BEST FRIEND'S RIDE

JULY 03, 2012

COMMENTS

MATT: Dax's Starship Alpha design is great. He did a bunch of designs, but I liked this one partly because it seemed the least aerodynamic (which, when you think about it, is not really an issue in space anyway).

DAX: This, I believe, was the official start of season two.

ROUGH LAYOUT

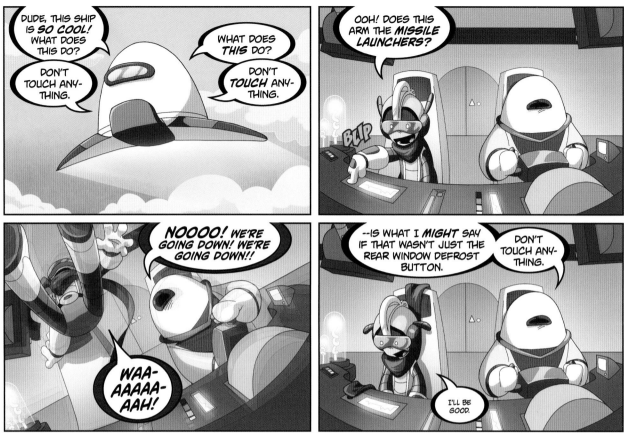

#036: PASSENGER SIDE

JULY 05, 2012

COMMENTS

MATT: Love the Starship Alpha interior as well. We'll see plenty more of the ship interior later on.

DAX: Starship Alpha is fun, am I right? P.S.: Don't push that one...

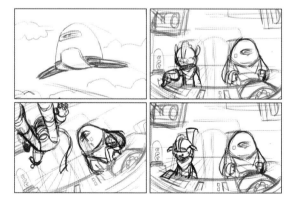

ROUGH LAYOUT

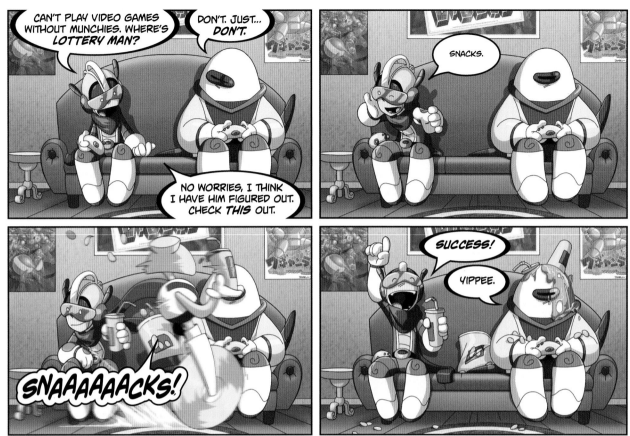

#037: SKILLFUL SNACKING

COMMENTS

MATT: Looks like Bravoman's got a handle on Lottery Man. Alpha… still not so much.

DAX: Fun fact: The Bravoman in panel four was blown up as a 30-foot banner for the last two San Diego Comic-Cons, advertising ShiftyLook's freeplay arcade!

ROUGH LAYOUT

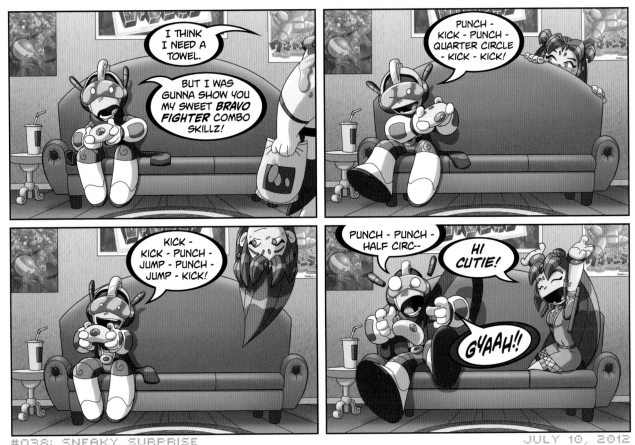

#038: SNEAKY SURPRISE

JULY 10, 2012

COMMENTS

MATT: I always like when we can have Waya doing sneaky ninja-esque things.

DAX: <3 Waya.

ROUGH LAYOUT

#039: PESTERING PRINCESS

COMMENTS

MATT: I think this might be the point where Waya unofficially shifts from a murderous enemy who happens to love Bravoman to an annoyingly lovesick friend who happens to want to kill Bravoman. It's a subtle difference.

DAX: I enjoyed drawing Waya in this strip as well as her interaction with Bravo. These kinds of polar opposite attitudes make for some fun posing and laughs.

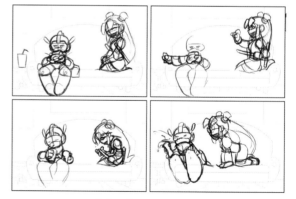

ROUGH LAYOUT

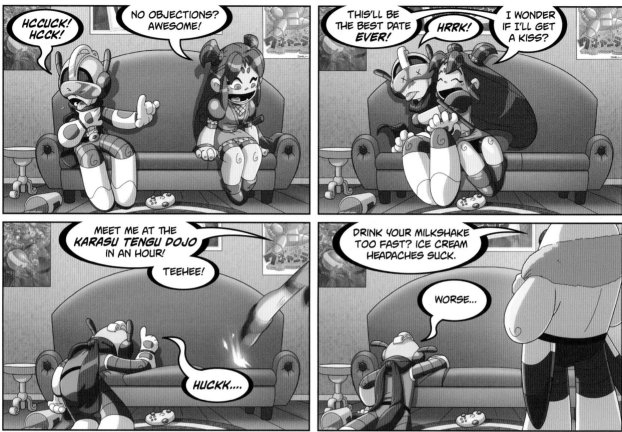

#040: HCKKK!

JULY 14, 2012

COMMENTS

MATT: When someone is choking is usually the best time to ask them out on a date.

DAX: I think I've redrawn this hug pose in one *Waya* or another five or so times during this series. #charm #history

ROUGH LAYOUT

#041: FORGOTTEN

JULY 17, 2012

COMMENTS

MATT: D'awww… poor little guy… but I bet we can be even meaner next time!

DAX: You know the writer is doing something right if even I felt bad working on this one… There is another strip that's worse, but we will get to it later.

ROUGH LAYOUT

#042: UH-OH AT THE DOJO

JULY 19, 2012

COMMENTS

MATT: The Tengu turned out really great. Both cute and scary!

DAX: That temple was hard to draw… Gimme characters any day of the week. :P

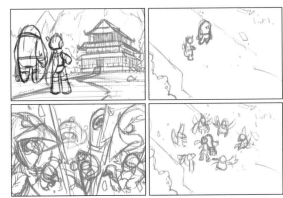

ROUGH LAYOUT

#043: ALPHA LOGIC

JULY 21, 2012

COMMENTS

MATT: This is totally just me Googling "Do crows have any natural predators?" and going "Oh, owls? Owl joke it is!"

DAX: I'm not sure if it was my idea to have Bravo break the fourth wall here, but I like that we are able to do that in this series. I think it's just another thing that gives it that #charm and brings readers into the fold.

ROUGH LAYOUT

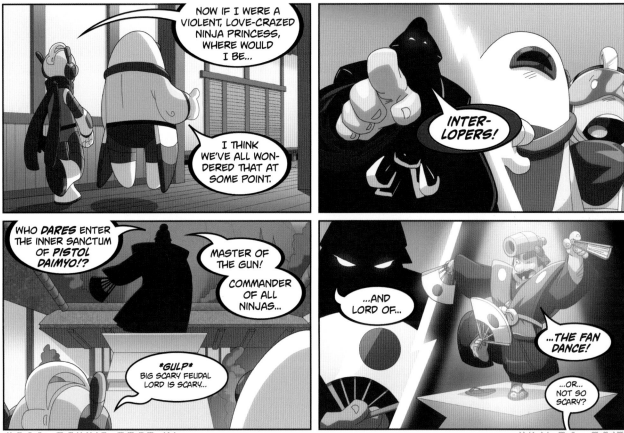

#044: DAIMYO DROP-IN

JULY 24, 2012

COMMENTS

MATT: Pistol Daimyo was one of the bosses from the original *Bravoman* game. In the game, he floats around by waving fans with his hands and feet. We brought him down to Earth a bit for the comic version, but I'm glad we kept a reference to the old-school goofiness.

DAX: Pistol Daimyo!!! Luckily, I haven't had to draw him doing the fan dance too many times… but as a throwback to the original game, I dig it.

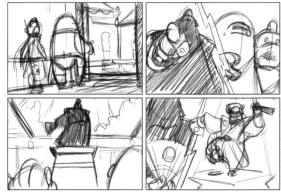

ROUGH LAYOUT

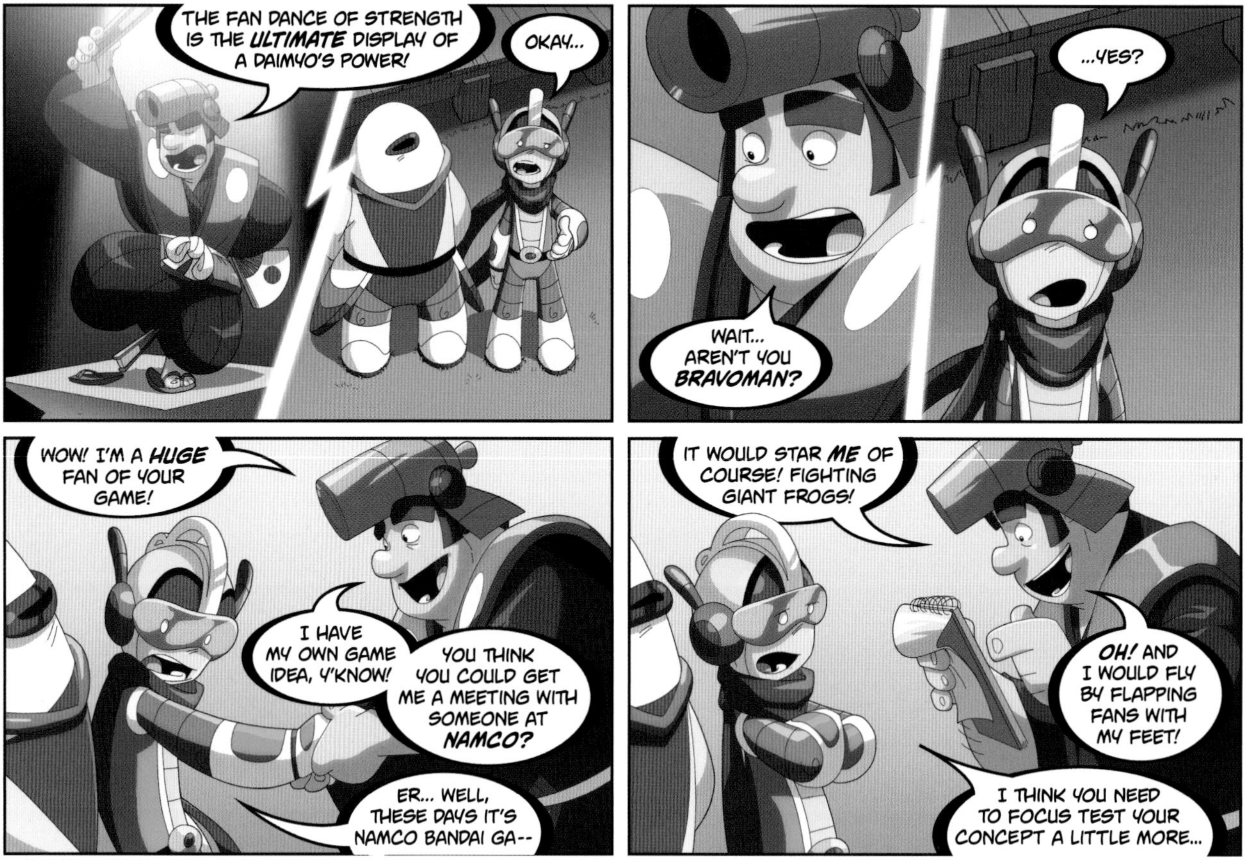
THE FAN DANCE OF STRENGTH IS THE ULTIMATE DISPLAY OF A DAIMYO'S POWER!
OKAY...
...YES?
WAIT... AREN'T YOU BRAVOMAN?
WOW! I'M A HUGE FAN OF YOUR GAME!
I HAVE MY OWN GAME IDEA, Y'KNOW!
YOU THINK YOU COULD GET ME A MEETING WITH SOMEONE AT NAMCO?
ER... WELL, THESE DAYS IT'S NAMCO BANDAI GA--
IT WOULD STAR ME OF COURSE! FIGHTING GIANT FROGS!
OH! AND I WOULD FLY BY FLAPPING FANS WITH MY FEET!
I THINK YOU NEED TO FOCUS TEST YOUR CONCEPT A LITTLE MORE...

#045: SUPER FAN

JULY 26, 2012

COMMENTS

MATT: Waya Hime, Anti-Bravoman, Pistol Daimyo... I seem to have an ongoing theme of antagonists who actually really like the hero, heh. While Anti-Bravoman both hates and secretly idolizes Bravoman as a hero, Pistol Daimyo is more of a Bravoman fanboy who sees our hero as a stepping stone for his own nerdy dreams. He is totally NOT like anyone I have met during my 10+ years working in the comics industry.

DAX: I always like drawing Pistol Daimyo. His face mostly, as I'm a sucker for huge eyebrows and he's one of the only *Bravoman* characters with a nose. ;P Fun fact: Notice how all the heroes don't have noses and the villains do?

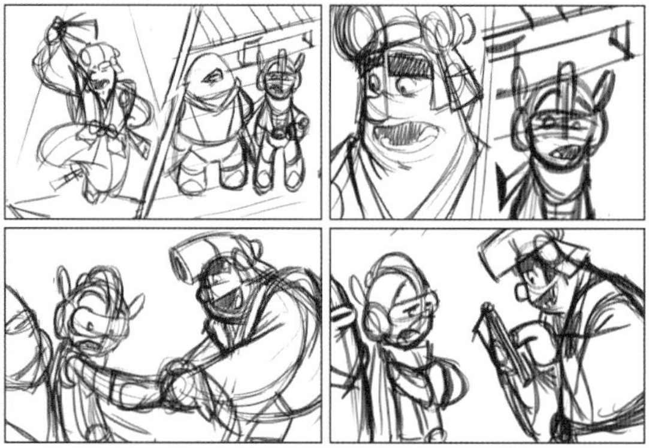

ROUGH LAYOUT

#046: SAVE THE PRINCESS!

COMMENTS

MATT: I've seen a few fans surmise that Pistol Daimyo is Waya Hime's father, but he is actually just the guy in charge of the ninjas, the Tengu, and the Karasu Tengu Dojo.

DAX: Panel three = fun to draw, and also one of the most memorable Waya Hime lines so far.

ROUGH LAYOUT

#047: SAVE THAT OTHER GUY!

JULY 31, 2012

COMMENTS

MATT: I had to color this strip myself for some emergency reason. I hope it looks roughly similar to Josh's standard super-dee-duper coloring skills.

DAX: Oh, Alpha… always getting in trouble.

ROUGH LAYOUT

#048: TRIVIAL TOWER

COMMENTS

MATT: Boy, that tower looks like it would have been an exciting adventure! Too bad Bravo ruined it...

DAX: Super fun and super fourth wall-breaking of extreme awesomeness. Why is there now a tower there? Just 'cuz.

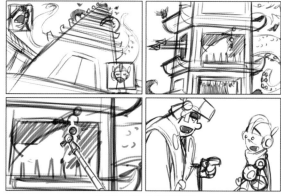

ROUGH LAYOUT

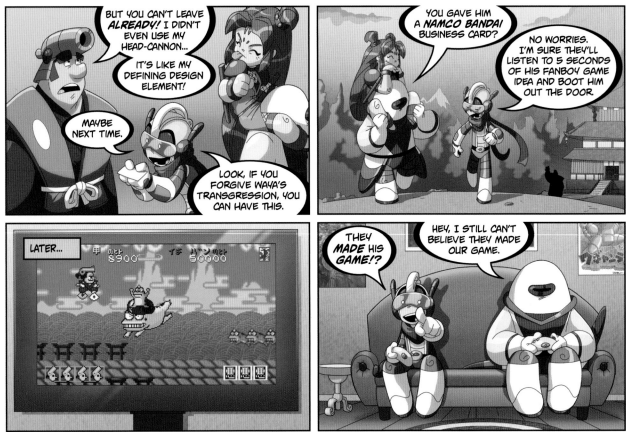

#049: DAIMYO DEALINGS

AUGUST 07, 2012

COMMENTS

MATT: So in reality, Pistol Daimyo did get his own spin-off game back in 1990! It was a Japan-exclusive arcade title, and that's a real screenshot. I daresay the game is even stranger than *Bravoman* was.

DAX: One of my favorite Waya drawings in the series. Just another chance to show her smitten with our hero.

ROUGH LAYOUT

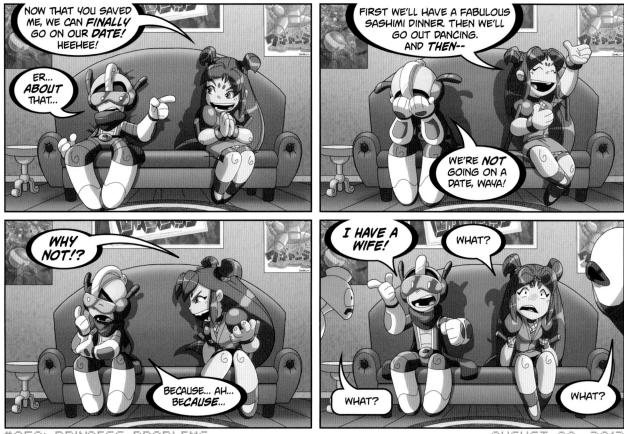

#050: PRINCESS PROBLEMS   AUGUST 09, 2012

COMMENTS

MATT: ...what!?

DAX: Bipolar much?

ROUGH LAYOUT

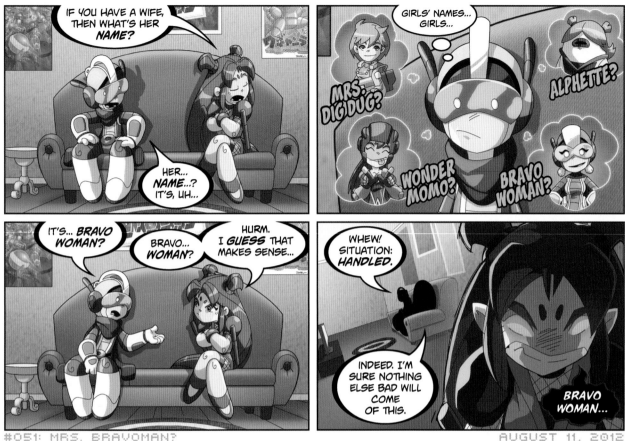

#051: MRS. BRAVOMAN?

COMMENTS

MATT: So we've got Bravo Woman, Alpha in a wig, Wonder Momo (the star of one of ShiftyLook's other top comics), and Mrs. Dig Dug, AKA Kissy from the game *Baraduke*.

DAX: This is Rob Pereyda's favorite strip. He tells me all the time. I think it has to do with the cameos of other Namco Bandai characters, which were a lot of fun to draw! I always like when cameo strips show up on my desk. This is also where I started playing with the dark side of Waya's character (a throwback to another game I spent a lot of time playing back in the day...).

ROUGH LAYOUT

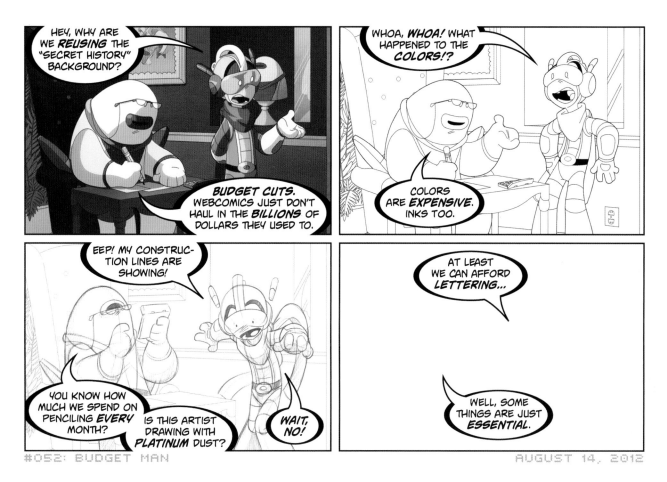

Panel 1:
HEY, WHY ARE WE *REUSING* THE "SECRET HISTORY" BACKGROUND?

BUDGET CUTS. WEBCOMICS JUST DON'T HAUL IN THE *BILLIONS* OF DOLLARS THEY USED TO.

Panel 2:
WHOA, *WHOA!* WHAT HAPPENED TO THE *COLORS!?*

COLORS ARE *EXPENSIVE.* INKS TOO.

Panel 3:
EEP! MY CONSTRUCTION LINES ARE SHOWING!

YOU KNOW HOW MUCH WE SPEND ON PENCILING *EVERY* MONTH?

IS THIS ARTIST DRAWING WITH *PLATINUM* DUST?

WAIT, NO!

Panel 4:
AT LEAST WE CAN AFFORD *LETTERING...*

WELL, SOME THINGS ARE JUST *ESSENTIAL.*

#052: BUDGET MAN   AUGUST 14, 2012

COMMENTS

MATT: One of my very favorite strips. The one-off strips that play with the medium are always the most fun to write.

DAX: I can't say it enough... this strip was super fun to do. Such a cool concept. Fun fact: Notice Alpha in panel three wearing reading glasses. ;)

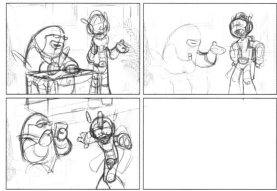

ROUGH LAYOUT

#053: FIENDISH FIGURES

AUGUST 16, 2012

COMMENTS

MATT: Eagle-eyed readers might notice the designs for an upcoming villain on the viewscreen there. We do plan things in advance… sometimes…

DAX: Hoverbot is now a permanent fixture in Dr. Bomb's lair. Always hovering and taking abuse…

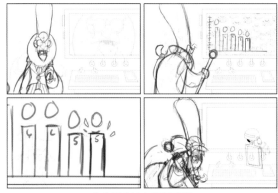

ROUGH LAYOUT

#054: R.C.M.

AUGUST 18, 2012

COMMENTS

MATT: Random Character Matchup has been a nice way to check in with characters we haven't seen for a bit. Often they almost write themselves; just put two characters together and let them do as they may.

DAX: RCM!!! Another cool idea by Matt (he has lots) and also a revisit to Bravo Woman, who now has a softer and more rounded look due to my constant evolution of the series' art.

ROUGH LAYOUT

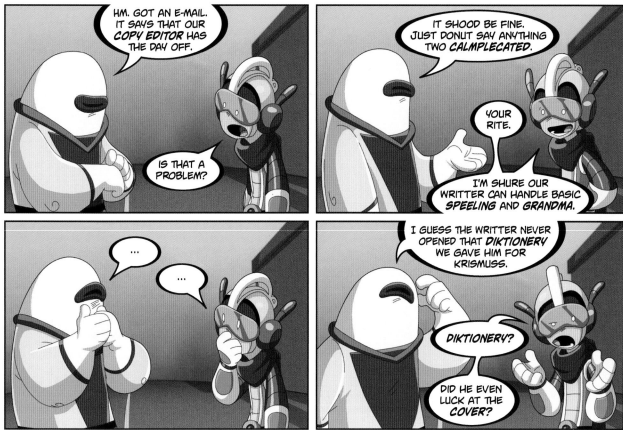

#055: GOOD WRITTING

AUGUST 21, 2012

COMMENTS

MATT: *Bravoman* is actually a side project for me. My regular job is working as UDON Entertainment's managing editor. It's amazing how often we will get an e-mail from a "professional writer" looking for work.

DAX: 'Nuff said.

ROUGH LAYOUT

#056: ANTI-BROODING

AUGUST 23, 2012

COMMENTS

MATT: For the first time we see Anti-Bravoman's bedroom, and really solidify his identity as an angsty teenager (though we will eventually learn that he is much younger than that). This is also when we started connecting the dots of his father/son relationship with Dr. Bomb.

DAX: In panel one, I added some toys to the bedroom... and spawned an entire set of retro toy catalog strips. *laughs*

ROUGH LAYOUT

COMMENTS

MATT: Another simple one-off strip I love. If you want to be a webcomic writer, just fill in the blanks – it's really that easy!

DAX: Bravoman was rarely seen in full profile before this point because I wasn't sure how to handle his noseless face from the side… Clearly it didn't work, and I eventually adopted a more anime profile for his character.

ROUGH LAYOUT

#058: A BRAVE FAN

COMMENTS

MATT: The first appearance of Brave Man! Bravoman's most hated nemesis!

DAX: Loved drawing this kid as I got to do the "Geeee mister, you're really strong!" thing.

ROUGH LAYOUT

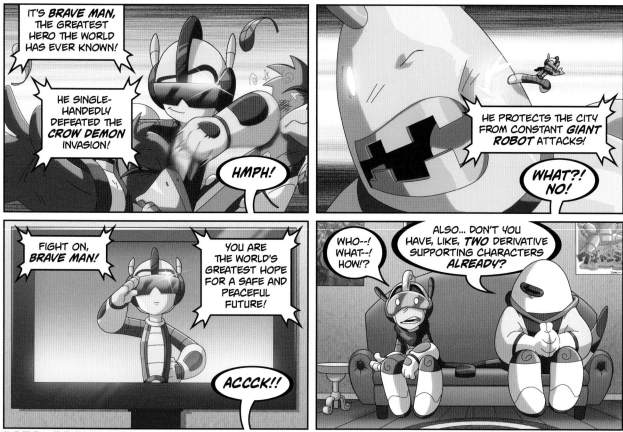

#059: BRAVE MAN

AUGUST 30, 2012

COMMENTS

MATT: So, the real scoop behind Brave Man is that he's based on the design you see in the box art used for the North American release of the *Bravoman* TurboGrafx-16 port. For whatever reason, they chose to redesign/recolor him for that artwork. He's basically the Bravoman equivalent of **Bad Box Art Mega Man**.

DAX: Such a cool idea here. I remember Matt telling me about it and thinking, "This'll be fun."

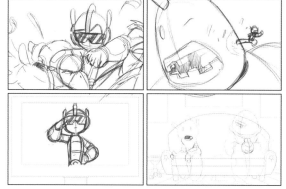

ROUGH LAYOUT

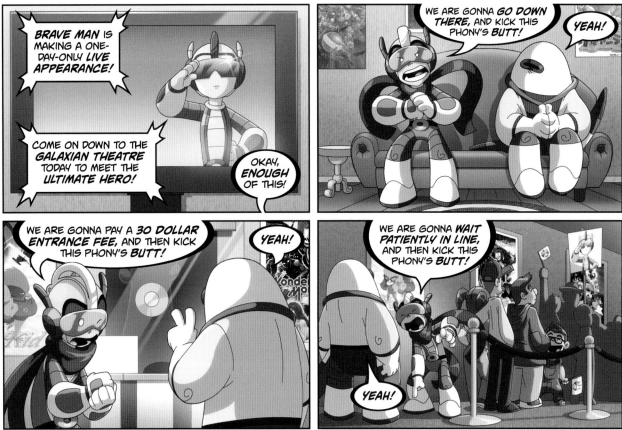

#060: BRAVOMAN WITH A PLAN

SEPTEMBER 01, 2012

COMMENTS

MATT: Repetition is always a useful weapon to have in your comedy war chest. Repetition is always a useful weapon to have in your comedy war chest. Repetition is ALWAYS a useful weapon to have in your comedy war chest.

DAX: That might be me as a kid in the line… just realized that. *laughs*

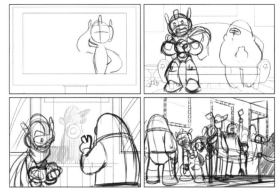

ROUGH LAYOUT

COMMENTS

MATT: Brave Man is the character who most irritates Bravoman. That he seems to do it so effortlessly makes him even more annoying.

DAX: Aww, Sally. Sometimes my favorite things to draw are the one-off characters.

ROUGH LAYOUT

#062: B-R-A-V-O SPELLS BRAVO!

SEPTEMBER 06, 2012

COMMENTS

MATT: In his early appearances, Brave Man's ear thingies were yellow. In later comics, they're red. I'd like to think that the marketing team at Brave Man Industries decided to make the change to better appeal to that key 18-35 age demographic... or, we just forgot or something.

DAX: Bravo shows he has an angry streak.

ROUGH LAYOUT

#063: BRAVE WORDS

SEPTEMBER 08, 2012

COMMENTS

MATT: Brave Man is just… so… frustrating! BRARRG!!

DAX: Nice callback to the first panel of *Bravoman* #1 here.

ROUGH LAYOUT

#064: LAWYERED

COMMENTS

MATT: The posters in the background are for other retro Namco Bandai properties. On the left is *Wrestleball* (known as *Powerball* in the West), *Dig Dug* is in the middle, and *Wagan Land* is on the right. *Wagan Land* is a Japanese-exclusive series about a robot dinosaur who solves puzzles and flies by spinning his head. I'm being super serious.

DAX: SLAM!

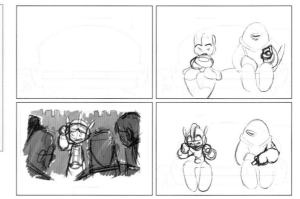

ROUGH LAYOUT

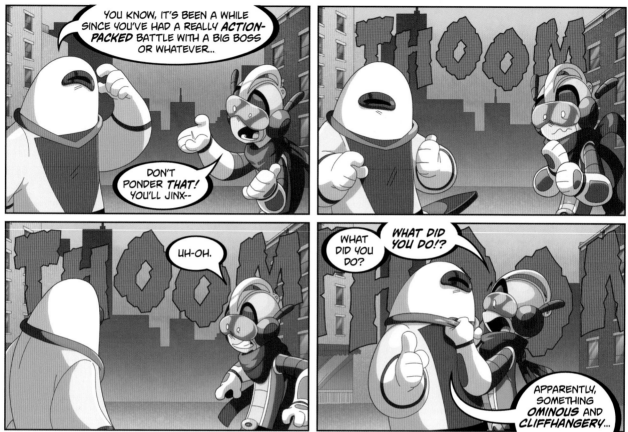

#065: THE START OF... SOMETHING!

SEPTEMBER 13, 2012

COMMENTS

MATT: Don't feel too bad, Alpha. Bravoman does almost the same thing a little down the road.

DAX: Another case where I had fun with the posing to express the growing fear in our heroic duo.

ROUGH LAYOUT

#066: ZOOORTAAAAN!

SEPTEMBER 15, 2012

COMMENTS

MATT: I'm not 100% sure what Zortan was supposed to be in the original game... some kind of robotic harpy? Anyway, Dax did a great job interpreting this odd character design. He's our first villain that is meant to seem truly menacing.

DAX: I remember really trying to push the FX in panel three to sell the power of the jump. Another example of/nod to my love of anime and its timing. Trying to capture that in the comic is a lot of fun.

ROUGH LAYOUT

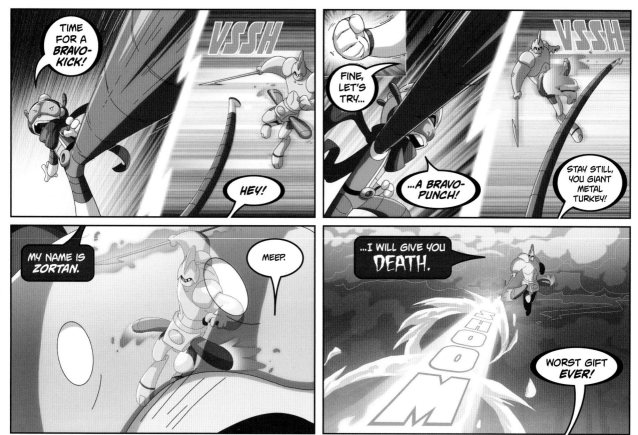

#067: BRAVO IN TROUBLE

SEPTEMBER 18, 2012

COMMENTS

MATT: The reflection in Bravo's visor is pretty slick. Way to go, art team!

DAX: One of my favorite action strips to this point. I was really able to push it and have fun. I believe the script said something like "Actiony stuff, punches and kicks that miss." As an artist I get a lot of freedom from Matt for these types of sequences, which is great.

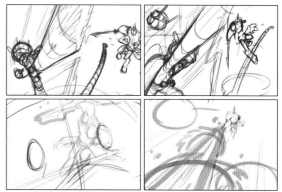

ROUGH LAYOUT

#068: SECRET POWER ACTIVE!

SEPTEMBER 20, 2012

COMMENTS

MATT: Bravoman officially gets his first new power! It won't be the last...

DAX: Something else I have used multiple times in the series is what I call the **pebble skip**, which is a huge shout-out to comic artist Joe Madureira. He was a massive influence on me growing up.

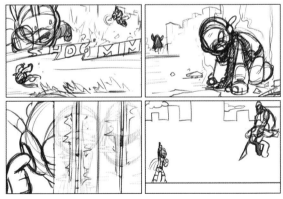

ROUGH LAYOUT

COMMENTS

MATT: The Bravo-Punch, Bravo-Kick, and Bravo-Headbutt are moves from the game. The Bravo-Buttbutt, that's all comic.

DAX: Buttbutt = win.

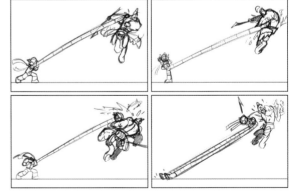

ROUGH LAYOUT

#070: BREAKING VARIOUS WALLS

SEPTEMBER 25, 2012

COMMENTS

MATT: The idea of reaching across the panel to get behind a bad guy's shield was the first joke I thought up when we were working on the initial pitch for *Bravoman*. I'm surprised it took me so long to actually use it!

DAX: The ultimate fourth wall gag. The idea of reaching across panels has been used a couple more times in the series since.

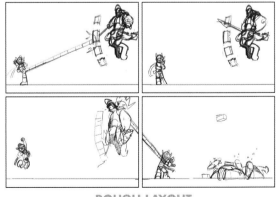

ROUGH LAYOUT

#071: IT FIGURES

SEPTEMBER 27, 2012

COMMENTS

MATT: This strip, as well as all the toy catalog strips we have done, was inspired by Dax drawing a few random action figures on the floor of Anti-Bravoman's bedroom in strip #56. Just goes to show that a small, random inclusion can have big effects on a mythos!

DAX: Uh-oh, here come the toys…

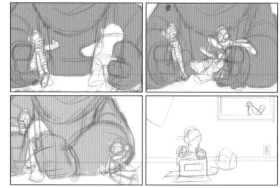

ROUGH LAYOUT

BRAVOMAN ACTION FIGURES!
SERIES 1

AS SEEN ON TG[16]

I TALK!

*recommended for ages 5 and up
(except ages 14-18, when kids go through that "too cool for toys" period)

BRAVOMAN 6-inch action figures are fully poseable, and fully awesome! Deluxe figures (items F-H) also include an exclusive BRAVOMAN mini-comic and activity book. Collect them all!

STANDARD ASSORTMENT:

A **BRAVOMAN** with NET LAUNCHERS and BANJO....................$7.99
B **ALPHA MAN** with SANDWICH and ALPHETTE DISGUISE......$7.99
C **WAYA HIME** with NINJA ARSENAL..$7.99
D **BENJAMIN** with KEYTAR SWORD $7.99
E **ANTI-BRAVOMAN** with TEDDY BEAR and PIGEON..............$7.99

DELUXE BRAVOMAN FIGURES:

F **SPACE ADVENTURE BRAVOMAN**.......................................$8.99
G **JUNGLE ATTACK BRAVOMAN**...$8.99
H **SUPER SURFIN' BRAVOMAN**...$8.99

OVERSIZED/PLAYSETS:

I **STARSHIP ALPHA**
Stores up to eight BRAVOMAN figures (sold separately)........$38.99
J **ATTACK BOMBER V9.1**
Says four different electronic phrases!
Requires fourteen AA batteries (not included)..........................$27.99

COMMENTS

MATT: The toy catalog strips are based off the ads you would see for toy lines in the Sears Christmas Wishbook during the 1980s. Google a few of them and you'll probably figure out some of the references we've made.

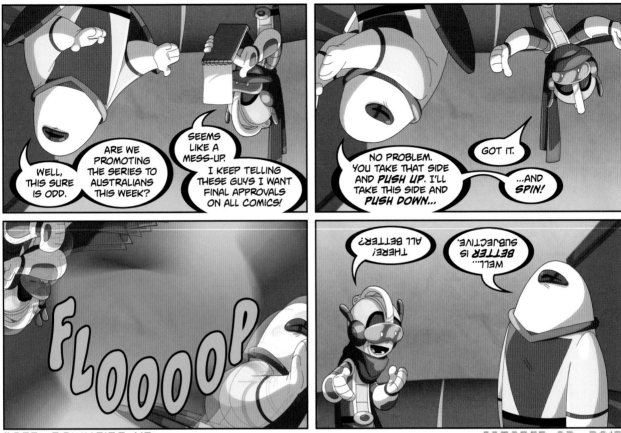

#073: DOWNSIDE UP

OCTOBER 02, 2012

COMMENTS

MATT: I like that Dax was clever enough to have Bravo's scarf hanging down; I wouldn't have thought of that.

DAX: Another weird one from Matt's brain... but fun to do!

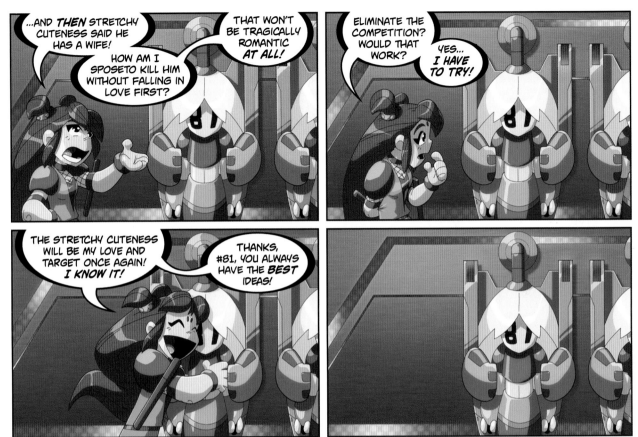

#074: WHINEY HIME

OCTOBER 04, 2012

COMMENTS

MATT: A little check-in with Waya Hime. Seems she likes to talk to Binjas when they're recharging... what a silly girl.

DAX: Gotta love Waya... but she's weird.

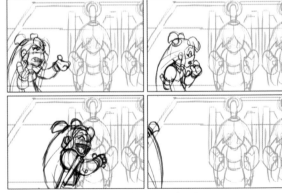

ROUGH LAYOUT

#075:
BRAVO X MOMO COVER
OCTOBER 06, 2012

GUEST ART BY:
EDWIN HUANG (LINE ART) &
ROB "ROBAATO" PORTER
(COLORS)

COMMENTS

MATT: This pinup was drawn by Edwin Huang *(Skullkickers)* and colored by Robaato *(Cryamore)*. Just a fun superhero style image to kick off our first intra-company crossover.

FYI, the **X** is pronounced **cross** in *Bravoman X Wonder Momo*'s title.
It's something of a tradition for Namco Bandai's video game crossovers.

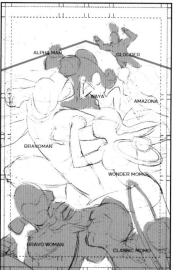

ROUGH LAYOUT

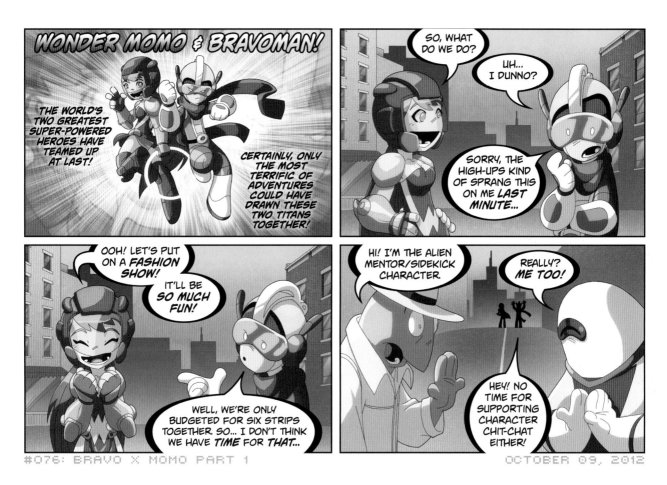

#076: BRAVO X MOMO PART 1

OCTOBER 09, 2012

COMMENTS

MATT: Bravoman and Momo do actually have some strong links going all the way back to their beginnings as 1980s Namco video game characters. They were both originally parodies of Japanese tokusatsu-style superheroes. Tokusatsu are Japanese live-action superhero shows with a lot of special effects, like *Kamen Rider* or *Ultraman*. Helmets like the ones Bravo and Momo wear are a staple of many tokusatsu heroes.

DAX: Loved working on this arc, as *Wonder Momo* is huge in Japan and on ShiftyLook. I also believe this is the first official crossover in ShiftyLook history!

ROUGH LAYOUT

#077: BRAVO X MOMO PART 2

COMMENTS

MATT: Bravoman and Wonder Momo have previously teamed up in the game *Namco X Capcom*. It was a Japan-exclusive tactical RPG for the PS2. It's too bad there's no English release; I'd love to give it a shot!

DAX: Can't believe we got this far in and Bravo is just now hearing A.B.'s name for the first time. :P #charm #history

ROUGH LAYOUT

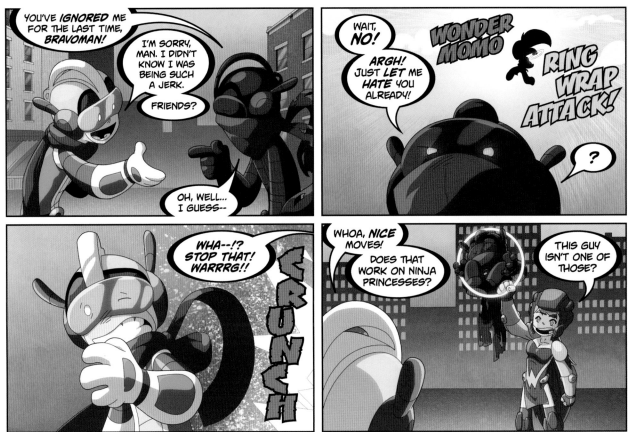

#078: BRAVO X MOMO PART 3   OCTOBER 14, 2012

COMMENTS

MATT: Come to think of it, Wonder Momo pulled the trigger pretty fast on attacking Anti-Bravoman... I guess that's just his lot in life.

DAX: I remember having fun with that silhouette in panel two. Took some time to get it right, but once I did I was happy.

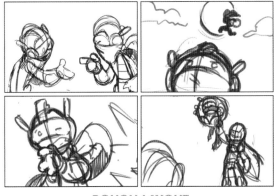

ROUGH LAYOUT

#079: BRAVO X MOMO PART 4   OCTOBER 16, 2012

COMMENTS

MATT: Coincidentally, the *Wonder Momo* webcomic eventually did a **Dark Momo** storyline. I guess Anti-Momo was just ahead of her time.

DAX: Designing Anti-Momo was super fun. It's a shame she was so short-lived!

#080: BRAVO X MOMO PART 5   OCTOBER 18, 2012

COMMENTS

MATT: For you non-nerds, *retcon* stands for *retroactive continuity*. It's a term for when changes are made to past stories for the sake of current ones. Retcons tend to be considered either lazy... or brilliant!

DAX: Oh, retcons.

ROUGH LAYOUT

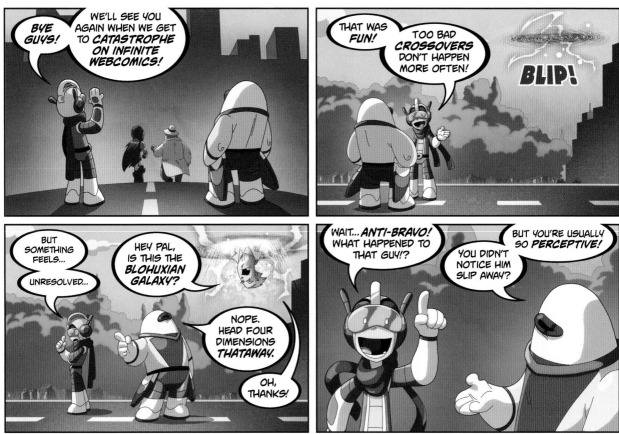

#081: BRAVO X MOMO EPILOGUE   OCTOBER 20, 2012

COMMENTS

MATT: The fellow in the portal is the surly lead character from another early ShiftyLook comic: *The Five-Dimensional Adventures of Dirk Davies*, by Ben McCool and Dean Haspiel. He's probably on the trail of a robot iguana serial killer or something.

DAX: Another fun cameo shows up in panel three, where Dirk Davies pops in to ask for directions.

ROUGH LAYOUT

#082: LOOK WHAT HAPPENS   OCTOBER 23, 2012

COMMENTS

MATT: Another one of those simple ideas that turned out great. Dax's animation background really shines with all those expressions. I rank this one among my favorite strips as well!

DAX: This was supposed to be a quick strip for me, as Matt said to just reuse some poses and draw a few more to sell the gag. This is a case where I got really into it by the fourth pose and started treating it like an animation scene that plays with Bravo's fun side.

ROUGH LAYOUT

#083: COMPLEX FORMULA

COMMENTS

MATT: There are all kinds of weird things snuck onto that blackboard. Some are jokes, some are gibberish... between these two strips, I'm sure you can figure out some of them. ;)

DAX: Probably my favorite pose of Dr. Bomb is seen in panel four. And clearly it is *evil math*.

#084: PLEASE?   OCTOBER 27, 2012

COMMENTS

MATT: More cementing of Dr. Bomb and Anti-Bravoman's father/angsty teenager relationship.

DAX: I don't usually have fun drawing inanimate objects, but this tank was definitely a rare time when I did. :)

ROUGH LAYOUT

AW! NOBODY TOLD ME THERE WAS A THEME...

#085: HAPPY HALLOWEEN!   OCTOBER 30, 2012

COMMENTS

MATT: I think we'll make the Hallowe'en strip an annual tradition. What costumes should we do THIS year, hmmm...

DAX: So, a few days before Hallowe'en, I say to Matt "We should do a special strip!" He says "Cool idea, go for it." I sent him this and the rest is #history!

ROUGH LAYOUT

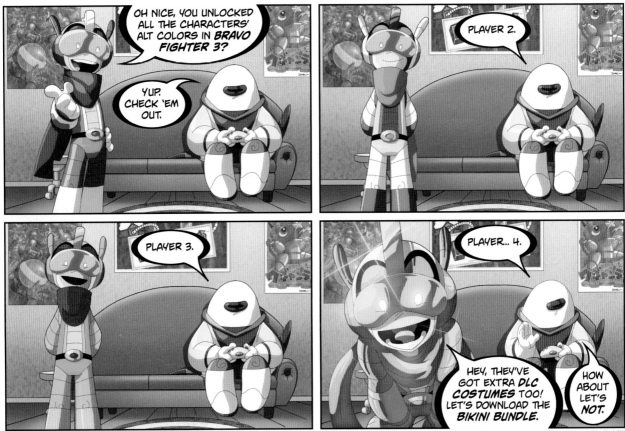

#086: ALT COLORS

NOVEMBER 01, 2012

COMMENTS

MATT: ShiftyLook asked if we could work in some alternate Bravoman colors into the strip, just in case we one day make some toys and need easy variant ideas. So here you go. (P.S.: I happen to know the episode Dax mentions below is called *The Golden Lagoon*... because I am a huge nerd.)

DAX: Gold Bravo reminds me of that one episode in *Transformers*, where they swim in the golden oasis... love it!

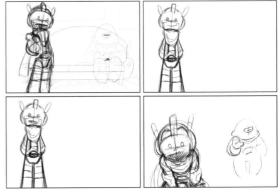

ROUGH LAYOUT

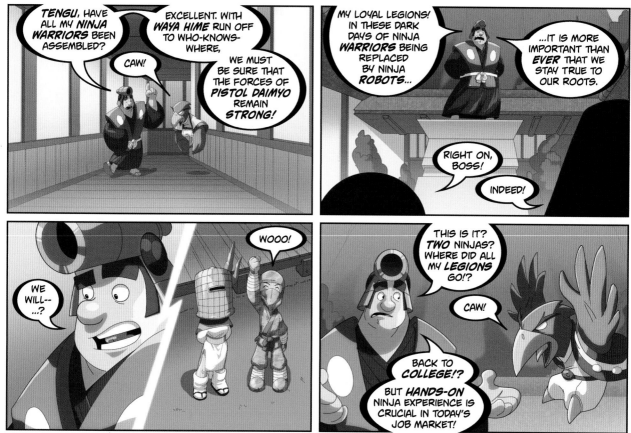

#087: DAIMYO'S DEARTH

NOVEMBER 03, 2012

COMMENTS

MATT: Camo and Komuso were created because I wanted to expand the ninja forces a bit. There are actually a lot of different types of ninjas in the classic *Bravoman* game. Camo is based on an enemy called Kakuremino, though Dax's version looks much cuter. Komuso is the actual name of another game enemy, but the game version usually stays completely hidden under her basket.

DAX: Fun stuff here, getting to design two more characters in our ever-expanding universe: Camo and Komuso!

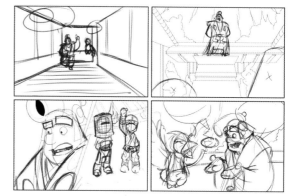

ROUGH LAYOUT

#038: ALWAYS BLEND IN

NOVEMBER 06, 2012

COMMENTS

MATT: I like characters who are super-enthusiastic, which is probably why I love Camo so much. We need to use him more often!

DAX: Camo is a guy who takes his visibility very seriously.

ROUGH LAYOUT

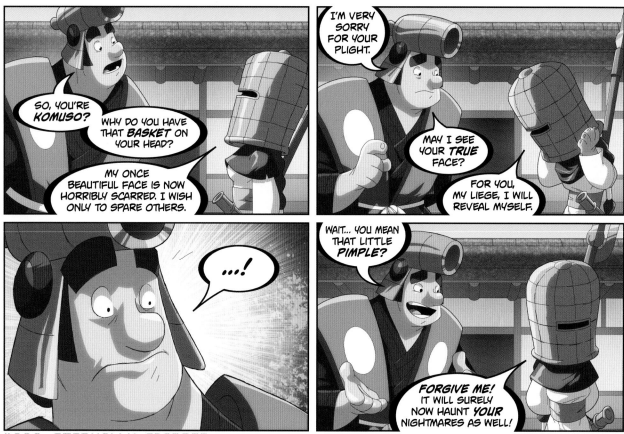

#089: ETERNALLY SCARRED

COMMENTS

MATT: Always good to add another girl to the roster. I kind of wanted Komuso to be the opposite of Waya Hime; someone who is reserved and takes things very seriously.

DAX: Komuso is fun, and I look forward to drawing her in future strips! I think we will have some fun with the whole faceless angle.

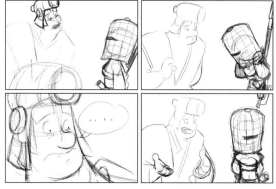

ROUGH LAYOUT

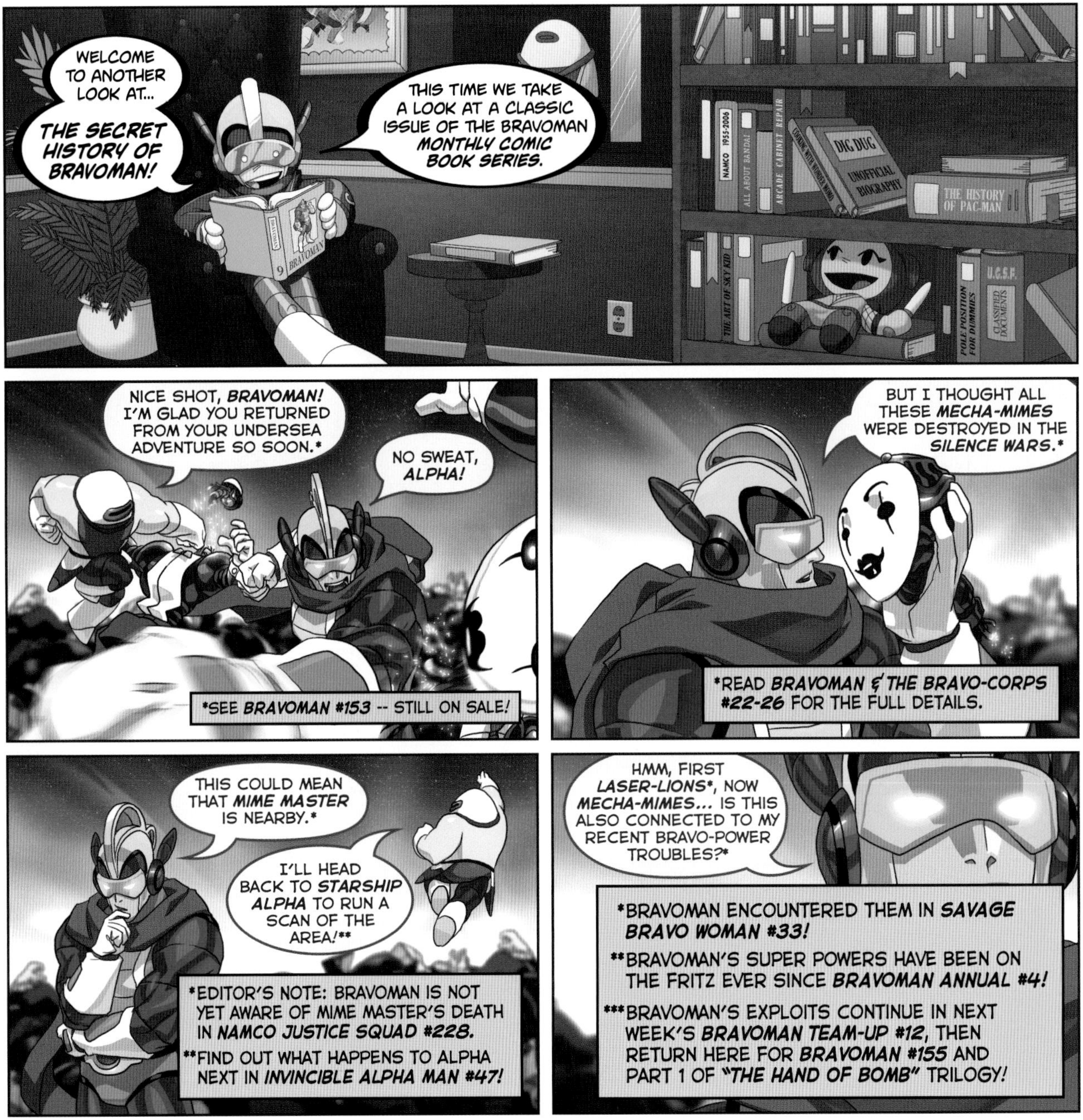

WELCOME TO ANOTHER LOOK AT... THE SECRET HISTORY OF BRAVOMAN!
THIS TIME WE TAKE A LOOK AT A CLASSIC ISSUE OF THE BRAVOMAN MONTHLY COMIC BOOK SERIES.
BRAVOMAN 9
NAMCO 1955-2006
ALL ABOUT BANDAI
ARCADE CABINET REPAIR
DIG DUG UNOFFICIAL BIOGRAPHY
THE HISTORY OF PAC-MAN
THE ART OF SKY KID
POLE POSITION FOR DUMMIES
CLASSIFIED DOCUMENTS
NICE SHOT, BRAVOMAN! I'M GLAD YOU RETURNED FROM YOUR UNDERSEA ADVENTURE SO SOON.*
NO SWEAT, ALPHA!
*SEE BRAVOMAN #153 -- STILL ON SALE!
BUT I THOUGHT ALL THESE MECHA-MIMES WERE DESTROYED IN THE SILENCE WARS.*
*READ BRAVOMAN & THE BRAVO-CORPS #22-26 FOR THE FULL DETAILS.
THIS COULD MEAN THAT MIME MASTER IS NEARBY.*
I'LL HEAD BACK TO STARSHIP ALPHA TO RUN A SCAN OF THE AREA!**
*EDITOR'S NOTE: BRAVOMAN IS NOT YET AWARE OF MIME MASTER'S DEATH IN NAMCO JUSTICE SQUAD #228.
**FIND OUT WHAT HAPPENS TO ALPHA NEXT IN INVINCIBLE ALPHA MAN #47!
HMM, FIRST LASER-LIONS*, NOW MECHA-MIMES... IS THIS ALSO CONNECTED TO MY RECENT BRAVO-POWER TROUBLES?*
*BRAVOMAN ENCOUNTERED THEM IN SAVAGE BRAVO WOMAN #33!
**BRAVOMAN'S SUPER POWERS HAVE BEEN ON THE FRITZ EVER SINCE BRAVOMAN ANNUAL #4!
***BRAVOMAN'S EXPLOITS CONTINUE IN NEXT WEEK'S BRAVOMAN TEAM-UP #12, THEN RETURN HERE FOR BRAVOMAN #155 AND PART 1 OF "THE HAND OF BOMB" TRILOGY!

#090: NOTE THE NOTES
GUEST ART BY JEFFREY CRUZ

NOVEMBER 10, 2012

#091: WOMAN WONDERINGS

NOVEMBER 13, 2012

COMMENTS

MATT: This is where we see the beginnings of Bravo Woman's frustrations at being a derivative female hero. When we brought her into the animated series, this is the aspect of the character we mostly chose to focus on.

DAX: Fun fact: Panel four is used heavily as reference in the *Bravoman* animated series episode *Perky Princess of Pointy Peril*.

ROUGH LAYOUT

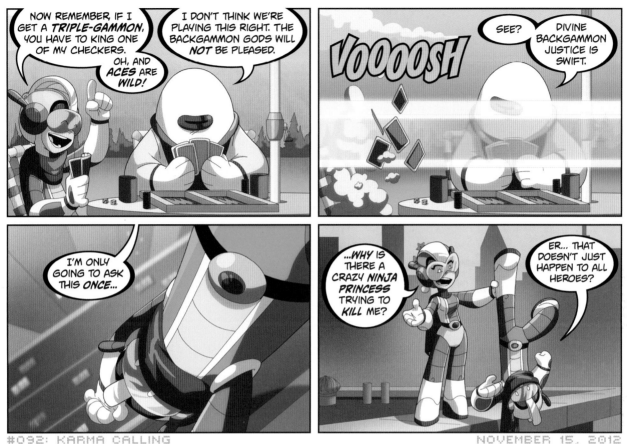

#092: KARMA CALLING

NOVEMBER 15, 2012

COMMENTS

MATT: Who doesn't love a good backgammon joke? Nobody, that's who.

DAX: I love the coloring on this one, as Josh really put a stamp on how Bravo Woman's flight trail looks.

ROUGH LAYOUT

#093: NINJA CHALLENGE   NOVEMBER 18, 2012

COMMENTS

MATT: This arc definitely has some of Dax's best action shots up to this point. It also makes use of a lot of split panels. These have become a staple in most of Dax's fight scenes so he can fit in more action beats. These days, for descriptions of panels like these, I'll generally just write to Dax: "Character X throws a bus at character Y. Split up the panels however much you need to."

DAX: A throwback to one of Waya's first confrontations with Bravo early on in the series (panel two). #charm #history

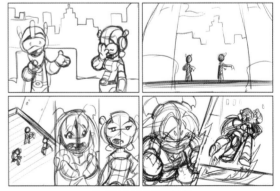

ROUGH LAYOUT

#094: TEST: FAILED

COMMENTS

MATT: I'd been saving the **Bechdel test** joke for a while, knowing that these two characters would eventually cross paths. It might be the snootiest joke I ever wrote.

DAX: I was in Japan, actually, working in the Namco Bandai head office during this arc. Such a great experience... one I will never forget!

ROUGH LAYOUT

#095: ACTION-HEAVY FILLER STRIP   NOVEMBER 22, 2012

COMMENTS

MATT: Love that first panel! Boy, they sure picked up a lot of speed falling off that building... good thing Bravo Woman was on the bottom to cushion the impact for Waya.

DAX: Definitely one of my favorite action strips! All kinds of actiony goodness!

ROUGH LAYOUT

#096: BRAVO COMES CLEAN

NOVEMBER 25, 2012

COMMENTS

MATT: Panel three is just great. Josh must have damaged his retinas coloring that one.

DAX: Huggggs!!!

ROUGH LAYOUT

#097: R.C.M. RETURNS

COMMENTS

MATT: Want to hear the translation of the joke? So do I!

DAX: Fun fact: Benjamin's pose was influenced by a friend of mine at ShiftyLook while I was in Japan. He was sitting across the table from me doing one of his impersonations/inside jokes, so I threw it in!

ROUGH LAYOUT

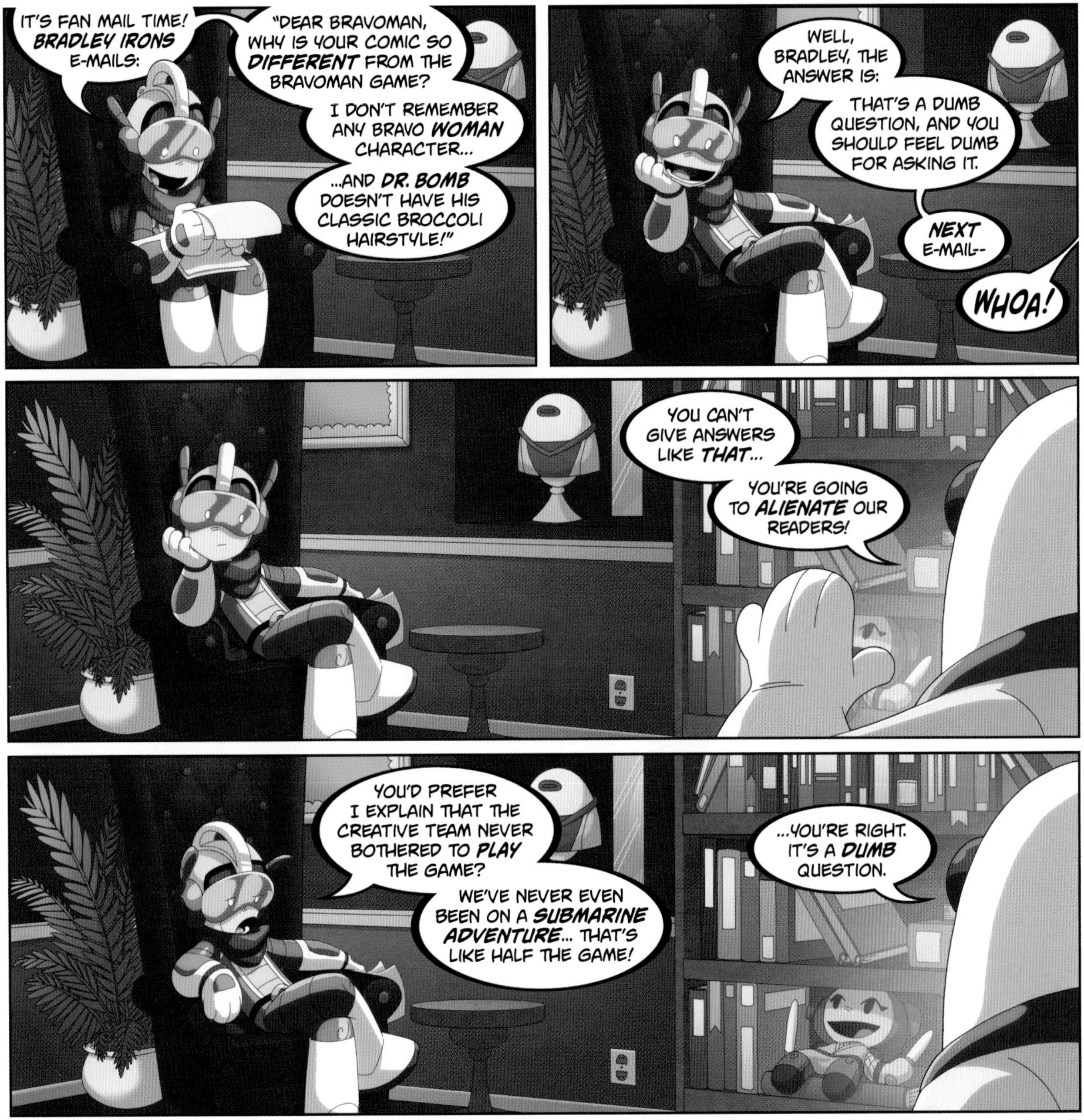
IT'S FAN MAIL TIME! BRADLEY IRONS E-MAILS:
"DEAR BRAVOMAN, WHY IS YOUR COMIC SO DIFFERENT FROM THE BRAVOMAN GAME?
I DON'T REMEMBER ANY BRAVO WOMAN CHARACTER...
...AND DR. BOMB DOESN'T HAVE HIS CLASSIC BROCCOLI HAIRSTYLE!"
WELL, BRADLEY, THE ANSWER IS:
THAT'S A DUMB QUESTION, AND YOU SHOULD FEEL DUMB FOR ASKING IT.
NEXT E-MAIL--
WHOA!
YOU CAN'T GIVE ANSWERS LIKE THAT...
YOU'RE GOING TO ALIENATE OUR READERS!
YOU'D PREFER I EXPLAIN THAT THE CREATIVE TEAM NEVER BOTHERED TO PLAY THE GAME?
WE'VE NEVER EVEN BEEN ON A SUBMARINE ADVENTURE... THAT'S LIKE HALF THE GAME!
...YOU'RE RIGHT. IT'S A DUMB QUESTION.

#098: MAILBAG

NOVEMBER 29, 2012

#099: ANTI-TANK - GUEST ART BY MATT MOYLAN   DECEMBER 01, 2012

I STILL HAVE TIME BEFORE BED!

WAHOO!

FINALLY SOME *REAL* EXCITEMENT!

#100: NUMBER 100!

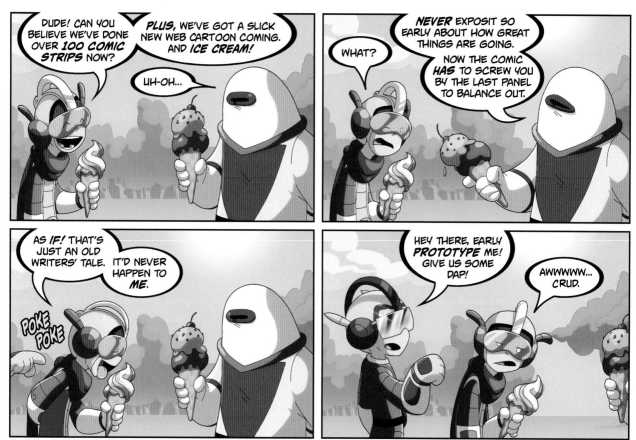

#101: BRAVO BALANCE

DECEMBER 06, 2012

COMMENTS

MATT: This little three-parter was done as a bit of housekeeping to get Brave Man out of the hands of those lawyers, so that we could include him in the next big story arc later on. Though I do like how it turned out.

DAX: Only Brave Man can ruin a good ice cream cone.

ROUGH LAYOUT

#102: FORTUNE FAVORS THE BRAVE

DECEMBER 08, 2012

COMMENTS

MATT: I think *parody* is cited a little too often these days as justification to play with other people's properties. Like, there's this guy who did a webcomic called *Lil Formers*, which obviously just sponged off of other popular properties. That guy was such a hack!

DAX: I like Matt's take on Brave Man, and the fact that Brave Man doesn't see how derivative he is. Again, supporting the theme of the web series. #charm #history

ROUGH LAYOUT

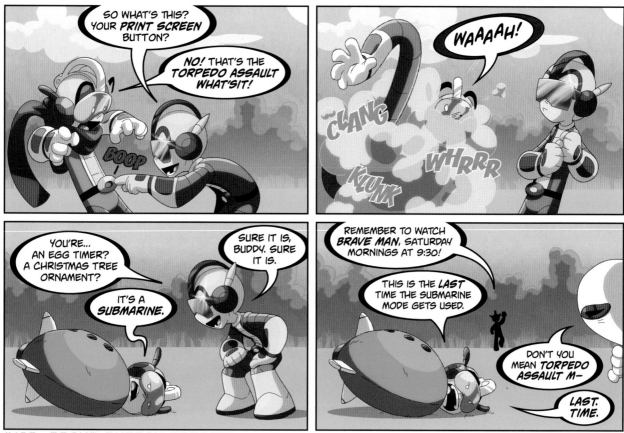

#103: BRAVE BUTTON-PRESSER

DECEMBER 11, 2012

COMMENTS

MATT: Only the second appearance of Bravoman's sub mode! Dax really disliked how goofy his first take on the sub design was, so Bravo is pretty much channeling Dax here. Dax ends up totally redesigning the sub mode for its next appearance.

DAX: This is the first strip where I had to do roughs on paper and then e-mail them for approval before finishing the final version via pics from an iPhone. I was in Singapore at the time, and I finished it in my hotel room.

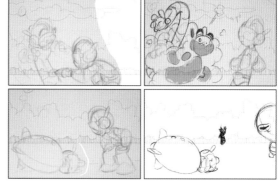

ROUGH LAYOUT

COMMENTS

MATT: Another in a series of blueprints I provided guest artwork for. The optional hippo-launcher is probably my favorite accessory on this particular mech.

DAX: Fun.

#105: LOVE-BOT - GUEST ART BY MATT MOYLAN   DECEMBER 16, 2012

COMMENTS

MATT: You shouldn't have left that pink crayon out where a girl could find it, A.B.

DAX: A.B. can't catch a break.

ROUGH LAYOUT

#106: THE RETURN   DECEMBER 19, 2012

COMMENTS

MATT: Hey, that's *Klonoa*! Why would you EVER return it!?

DAX: First strip back from Japan! And a fun concept to do.

ROUGH LAYOUT

#107: ANTI-BRAGGING   DECEMBER 20, 2012

COMMENTS

MATT: I really like this one; it grew so naturally from the strip where Bravoman defeats Zortan. Fourth wall-breaking, angry Waya Hime, Anti-Bravoman failing... it's got everything you could want from a *Bravoman* comic!

DAX: Waya's pose in panel one is just sooooo **her**.

ROUGH LAYOUT

'TIS THE SEASON FOR ALPHA CLAUS!

A LOCK OF HAIR FROM THE CUTIEST OF CUTE CUTIES!

DON'T TELL HIM I ENCOURAGED YOU.

7/8 INCH BOLTS! USEFULLY EXCELLENT!

HELICALLY-RIDGED FASTENERS ARE MY MOST *FAVORITE* METHOD OF AFFIXATION!

RIGHT... THAT STUFF YOU SAID.

SNAAAAAAACKS! I *LOVE* SNACKS!

NO KIDDING.

VAC-METAL GOLD BRAVOMAN!? BUT THIS WAS A CONVENTION *EXCLUSIVE!!*

ALPHA CLAUS LIKES TO PLAY THE SPECULATOR MARKET.

#108: ALPHA CLAUS PART 1

DECEMBER 23, 2012

COMMENTS

MATT: The X-mas strips were super fun to do too. Maybe we can keep them going each year by giving presents to the new characters.

DAX: It was a lot of fun to do the whole present thing. A great glimpse into everyone's character here.

ROUGH LAYOUT

#109: ALPHA CLAUS PART 2

DECEMBER 25, 2012

COMMENTS

MATT: I'm coming to realize that between the webcomic and the animated series, we've made a LOT of *Pac-Man* references... like, seriously.

DAX: Nicely done, Matt... great ending. He doesn't just do comedy, folks!

ROUGH LAYOUT

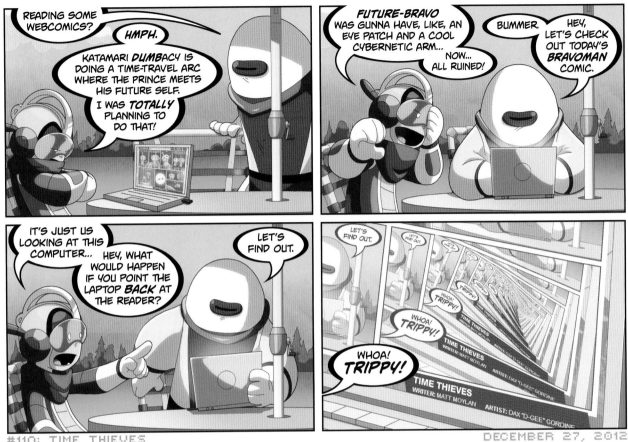

#110: TIME THIEVES

DECEMBER 27, 2012

COMMENTS

MATT: This might be my favorite strip, partly because I like how the last panel turned out. I don't think I have seen that particular visual gag done before in comics. But also, the *Katamari* guys beating us to the punch on doing a time travel story is totally true! Darn you, Buttersafe! *shakes fists threateningly* If you don't know, *Katamari* is another ShiftyLook webcomic created by the dynamic duo of Alex Culang and Ray Castro (collectively known as Buttersafe). I hope they read this, or else all that fist-shaking will have been really pointless.

DAX: Characters in the webcomic reading their own webcomic... madness! But awesome.

ROUGH LAYOUT

#111: REBIRDED

COMMENTS

MATT: Nega-Pigeon is the best character ever. He doesn't do ANYthing. He just hangs around Anti-Bravoman and acts like a pigeon. And people love him. Awesome.

DAX: Remember this little guy? Well, 100 or so strips later, Nega-Pigeon is born! We listened to fans; the proof is in the pigeon.

ROUGH LAYOUT

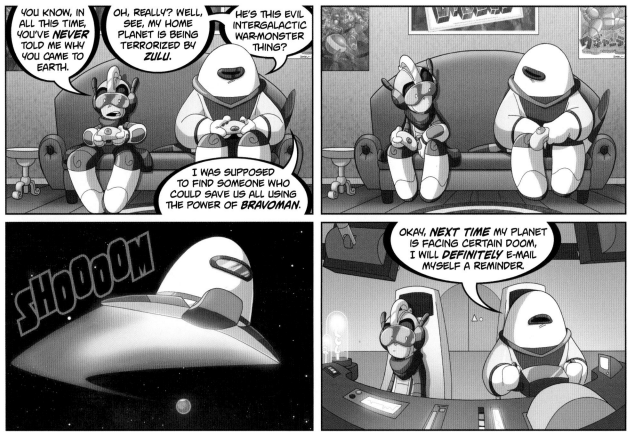

#112: MEMORY ALPHA

COMMENTS

MATT: This is totally one of those ideas that came out of a random thought popping into my head. "Why IS Alpha just goofing off on Earth playing video games with Bravoman? Doesn't he have anything better to do?" Oh, I guess maybe he does...

DAX: When I got the scripts for this arc, I laughed out loud. I'm a huge fan of the *take* - or pausing for a *beat* - in comedic situations. This was absolutely one of those times for me. I had a blast drawing panel two.

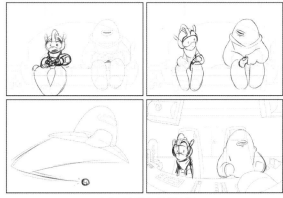

ROUGH LAYOUT

#113: SPACE JAM

JANUARY 03, 2013

COMMENTS

MATT: The traffic line in space. Such a *Jetsons* joke. Do kids still know what *The Jetsons* is? (Honestly, even I shouldn't really know what *The Jetsons* is...)

DAX: Originally I hated the thought of this strip, you know... all the spaceships and such... but in the end, I rather like how it turned out! I also think there are seven cameo ships in the traffic, can you spot 'em all?

ROUGH LAYOUT

#114: WELCOME TO PLANET ALPHA

JANUARY 05, 2013

COMMENTS

MATT: The Alpha Tower/Alpha Dome is a super-hidden reference to the city of Toronto, where I've lived for over ten years now. We don't have any giant cyber-octopuses, though, as far as I know.

DAX: Planet Alpha was fun and simplistic, which was great because I really enjoy letting the characters take center stage in all my work. Matt has definitely over time found a way to write that into these scripts very effectively.

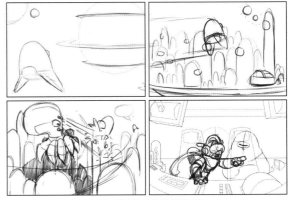

ROUGH LAYOUT

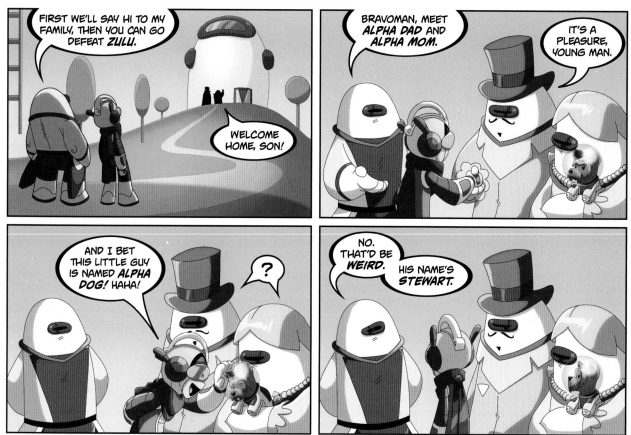

#115: ALPHAMILY

JANUARY 08, 2013

COMMENTS

MATT: So Planet Alpha is in imminent danger, but nobody seems to be super concerned about it. I guess all the other Alphans are just as calm and collected as Alpha Man.

DAX: Why wouldn't Alpha Dad wear a top hat? Oh, and Stewart is a Yorkshire Terrier. He is based off of my friend's little three-legged wonder pup, Oscar.

ROUGH LAYOUT

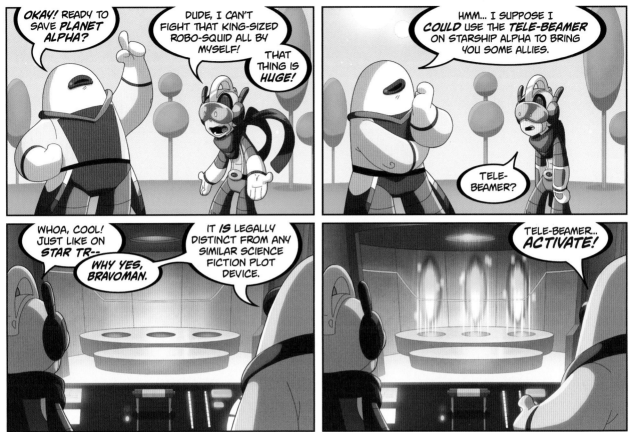

#116: IN NEED OF ALLIES

COMMENTS

MATT: *Legally distinct* is a very useful term.

DAX: Josh killed it with the *Star Trek*-style beaming FX in this one. His colors are always fantastic.

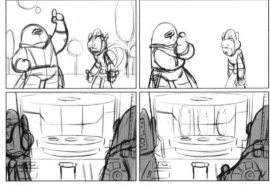

ROUGH LAYOUT

JANUARY 15, 2013

COMMENTS

MATT: I guess Bravo Woman was washing her... helmet?

DAX: A fun one because, again, I like to do anything that shows character and personality. Obviously we get to see a slice of that in each panel here.

ROUGH LAYOUT

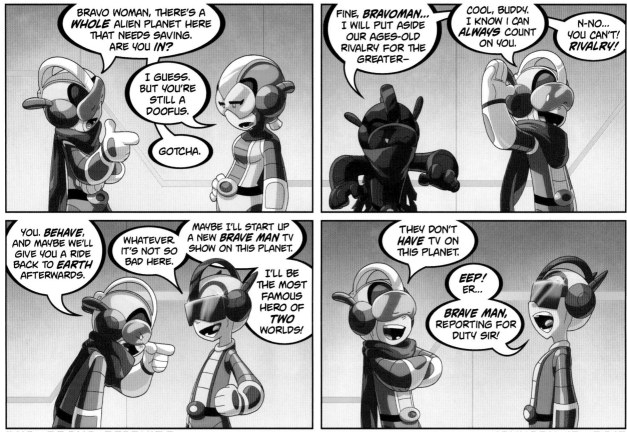

#118: BRAVO RECRUITS

JANUARY 17, 2013

COMMENTS

MATT: Bravoman pointing at Brave Man is my favorite panel here. He's just so, "You... how DARE you exist!"

DAX: For character, personality, and posing, this is my favorite strip to date. I like how Bravo goes through four completely different moods here. I really hope this scene makes it into an animated form someday, as I think it could work very well.

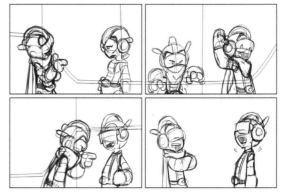

ROUGH LAYOUT

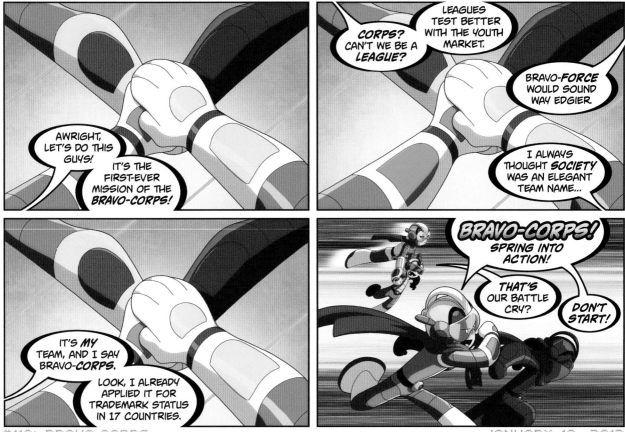

#119: BRAVO-CORPS

COMMENTS

MATT: Yeah! The formation of the Bravo-Corps! I'd been waiting for a chance to team everyone up ever since we added Bravo Woman and Brave Man to the cast.

DAX: Getting to spend most of your time on a fun, action-packed panel four!? Sure thing, sign me up! Action is always fun to do!

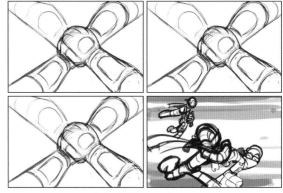

ROUGH LAYOUT

#120: ZULU'S WRATH

COMMENTS

MATT: Looks like there was a little miscoloring in this strip (Dax explains below), but I didn't notice at the time. Sometimes I'll just letter a strip from memory, so here I probably just rolled with it and assumed I meant for Anti-Bravoman to have some dialog in panel two.

DAX: Ok, here we get into the meat of the storyline! Bravo-Corps assemble! Fun fact: The first part of panel two was drawn as Bravoman (which is why his scarf isn't covering his mouth) because, in the script, he originally said something like "A.B., You tie up his legs while I..."

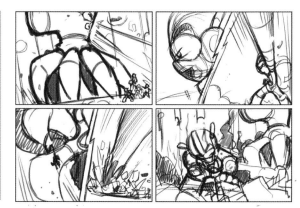

ROUGH LAYOUT

#121: WRATH OF ZULU   JANUARY 24, 2013

COMMENTS

MATT: Zulu is another great original character design from Dax! He came up with a pile of design ideas, which you can see in the sketch gallery at the back of the book.

DAX: The one and only time Brave Man is useful... as a distraction *laughs*... love it. Plus, I like that Bravo Woman is so strong, because we can really throw her around with fun action while still making it ***believable***.

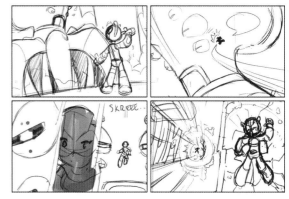

ROUGH LAYOUT

#122: CONTINUITY!   JANUARY 26, 2013

COMMENTS

MATT: This whole arc is built around creating a standalone story that doesn't stand alone; a technique I picked up from the manga series *Bakuman*. The trick is to go back through your past continuity, pick up various threads that seemed random at the time, and combine things to make it look like you were planning everything all along. A.B.'s anti-particles/merger powers is the most obvious example of that. They were originally just a one-off idea in the *Wonder Momo* crossover, but they've been brought back here in a big way!

DAX: I love the explanation of the anti-particles that started off with the *Bravo X Momo* arc! Nice work, Matt! Also loving Josh's smoke here… so anime!

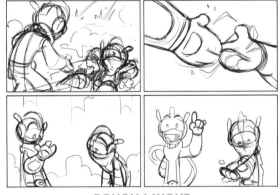

ROUGH LAYOUT

#123: SUCKS TO BE ANTI

JANUARY 29, 2013

COMMENTS

MATT: Anti-Bravoman gags are so often the ones where I have the two little Matts on my shoulders. Angel Matt: "OMG! That's SO mean! Who would write such a thing?" Devil Matt: "Sucks to be you, Anti-Bravoman! Haw haw!"

DAX: Okay, this is the strip I was referring to in a previous comment... I felt horrible while drawing this. *laughs* But I suppose that means A.B. is a character you actually feel for, which shows we are doing our job well, right? I also tried to reflect the angst in the faces of the three offenders in panel four. They didn't really WANT to do it. At least I feel that way.

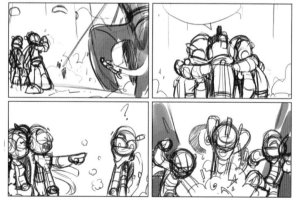

ROUGH LAYOUT

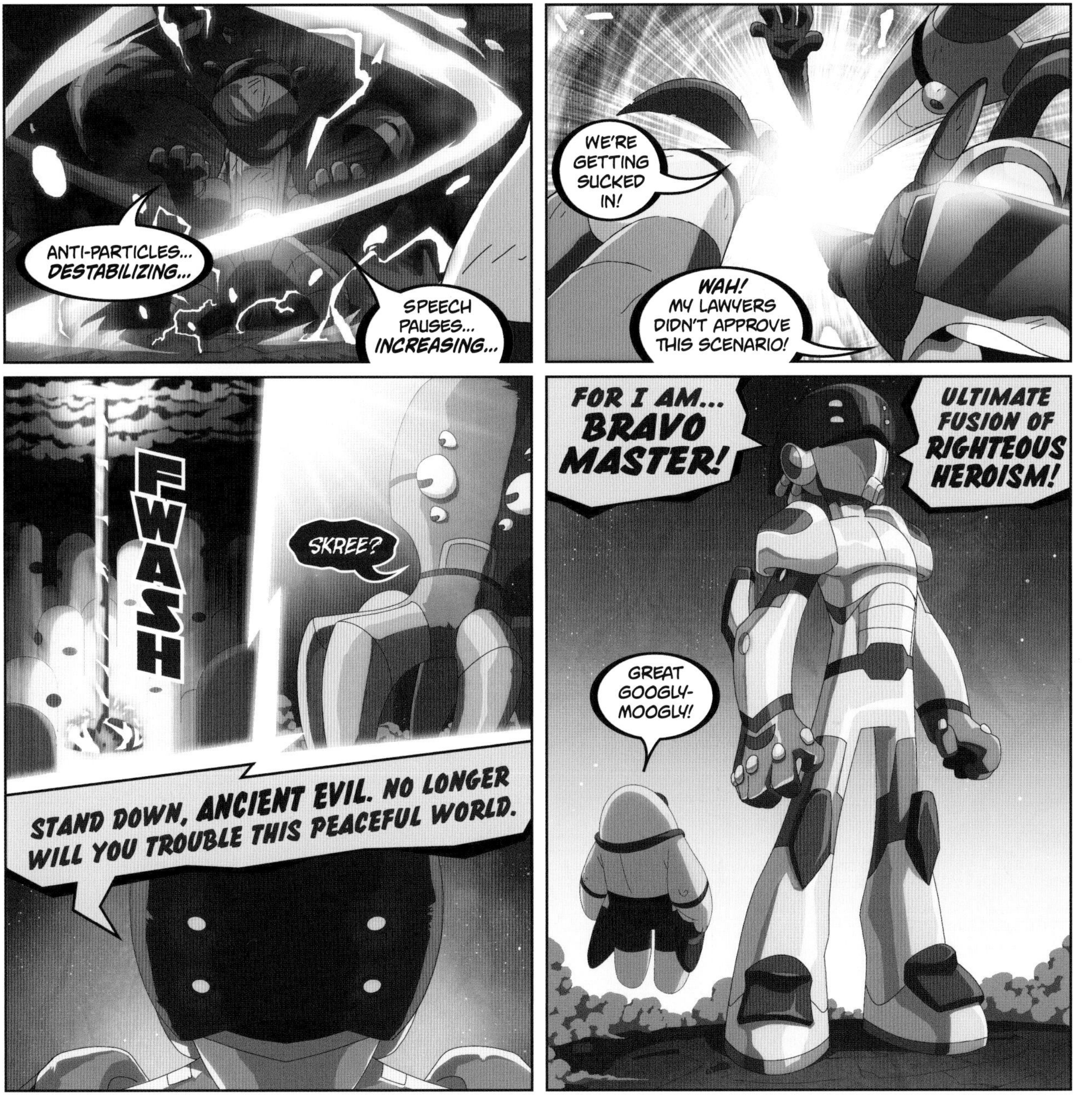
ANTI-PARTICLES... DESTABILIZING...
SPEECH PAUSES... INCREASING...
WE'RE GETTING SUCKED IN!
WAH! MY LAWYERS DIDN'T APPROVE THIS SCENARIO!
FWASH
SKREE?
STAND DOWN, ANCIENT EVIL. NO LONGER WILL YOU TROUBLE THIS PEACEFUL WORLD.
FOR I AM... BRAVO MASTER!
ULTIMATE FUSION OF RIGHTEOUS HEROISM!
GREAT GOOGLY-MOOGLY!

#124: BRAVULAR FUSION

JANUARY 31, 2013

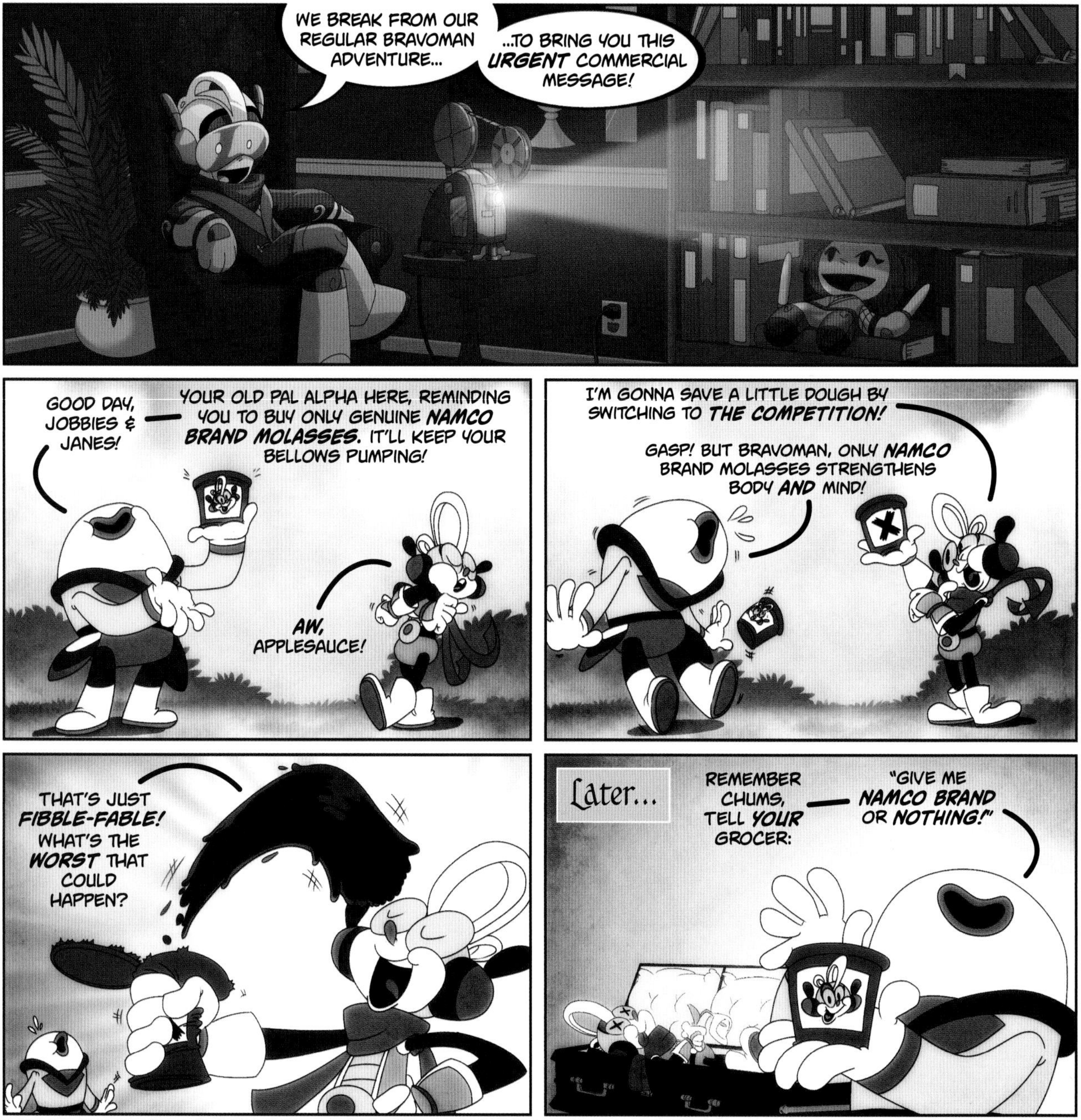
WE BREAK FROM OUR REGULAR BRAVOMAN ADVENTURE...
...TO BRING YOU THIS *URGENT* COMMERCIAL MESSAGE!
GOOD DAY, JOBBIES & JANES!
YOUR OLD PAL ALPHA HERE, REMINDING YOU TO BUY ONLY GENUINE *NAMCO BRAND MOLASSES.* IT'LL KEEP YOUR BELLOWS PUMPING!
AW, APPLESAUCE!
I'M GONNA SAVE A LITTLE DOUGH BY SWITCHING TO *THE COMPETITION!*
GASP! BUT BRAVOMAN, ONLY *NAMCO* BRAND MOLASSES STRENGTHENS BODY *AND* MIND!
THAT'S JUST *FIBBLE-FABLE!* WHAT'S THE *WORST* THAT COULD HAPPEN?
Later...
REMEMBER CHUMS, TELL *YOUR* GROCER:
"GIVE ME *NAMCO BRAND* OR *NOTHING!*"

#125: BRAVO BRANDING - GUEST ART BY JOSH PEREZ FEBRUARY 02, 2013

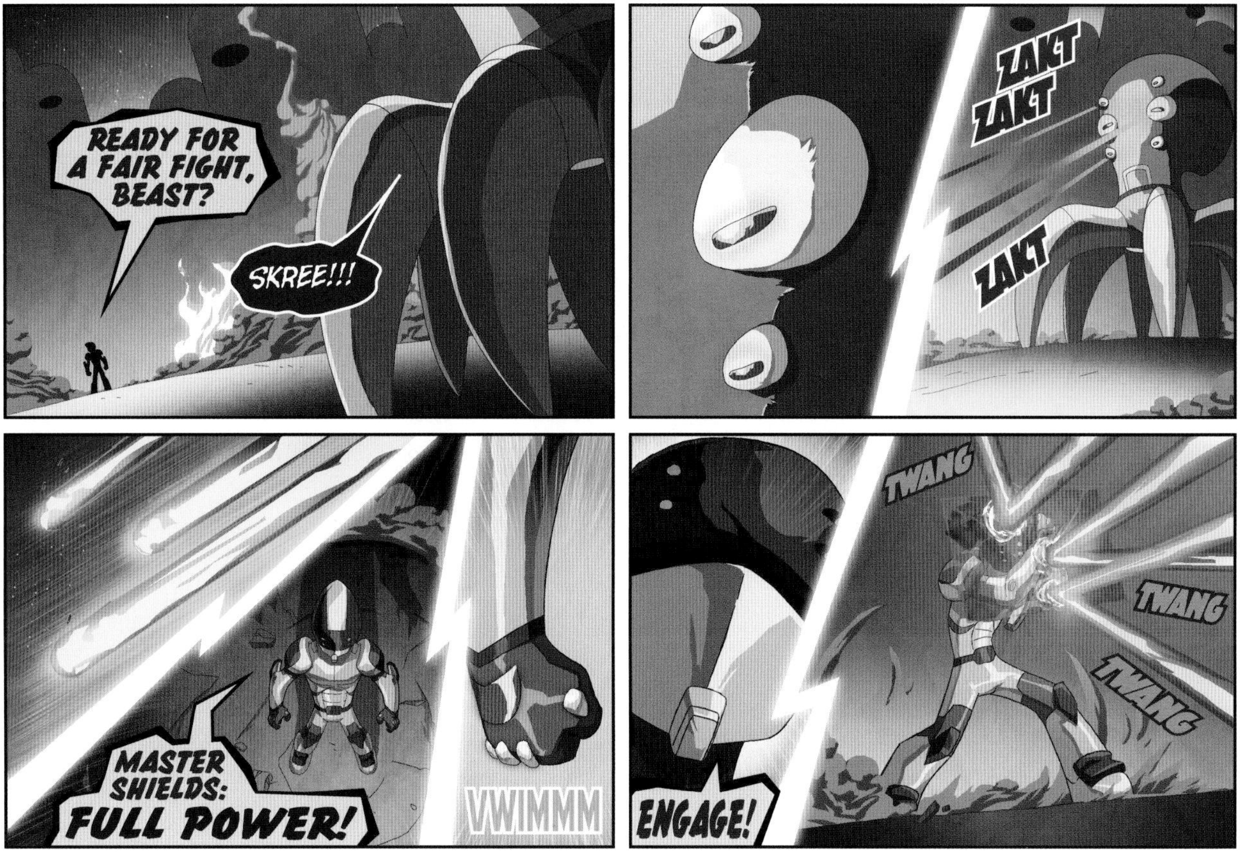
READY FOR A FAIR FIGHT, BEAST?
SKREE!!!
ZAKT
ZAKT
ZAKT
MASTER SHIELDS: FULL POWER!
VWIMMM
TWANG
TWANG
TWANG
ENGAGE!

#126: MANEUVER: X-RAY

FEBRUARY 05, 2013

COMMENTS

MATT: Bravo Master is totally not what I initially wrote him to be… he's WAY cooler now! But I'm going to keep my original idea in a drawer, I may still have a use for it down the road…

DAX: I had so much fun with the Bravo Master stuff and had a lot of input as to the origin and how he came to be. I wanted to make him bigger in scale to give it a more epic vibe. Fun fact: Bravo Master was scripted to just be the same size as our heroes.

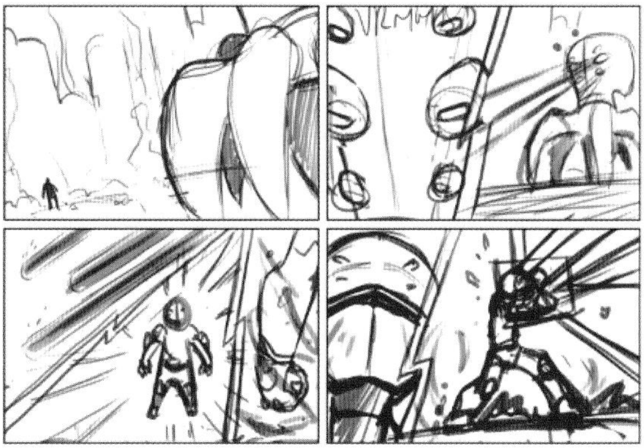

ROUGH LAYOUT

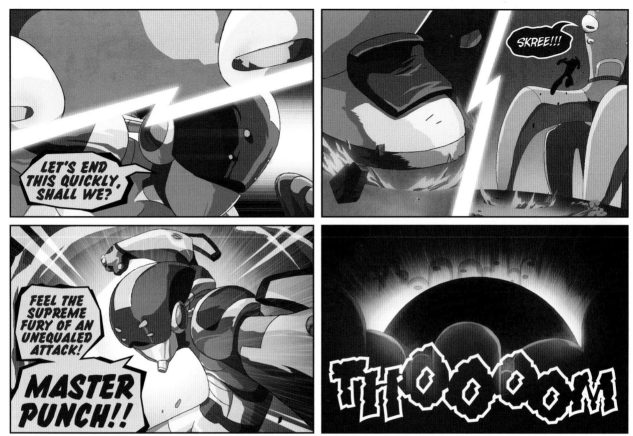

#127: MANEUVER: YANKEE

FEBRUARY 07, 2013

COMMENTS

MATT: That *Akira*-esque explosion turned out great.

DAX: Fun fact: The previous two strips were done as one big page, but were split in order to extend the action. They still read better as one piece in my opinion.

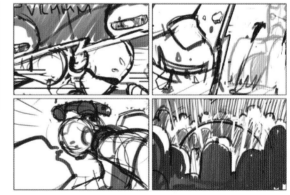

ROUGH LAYOUT

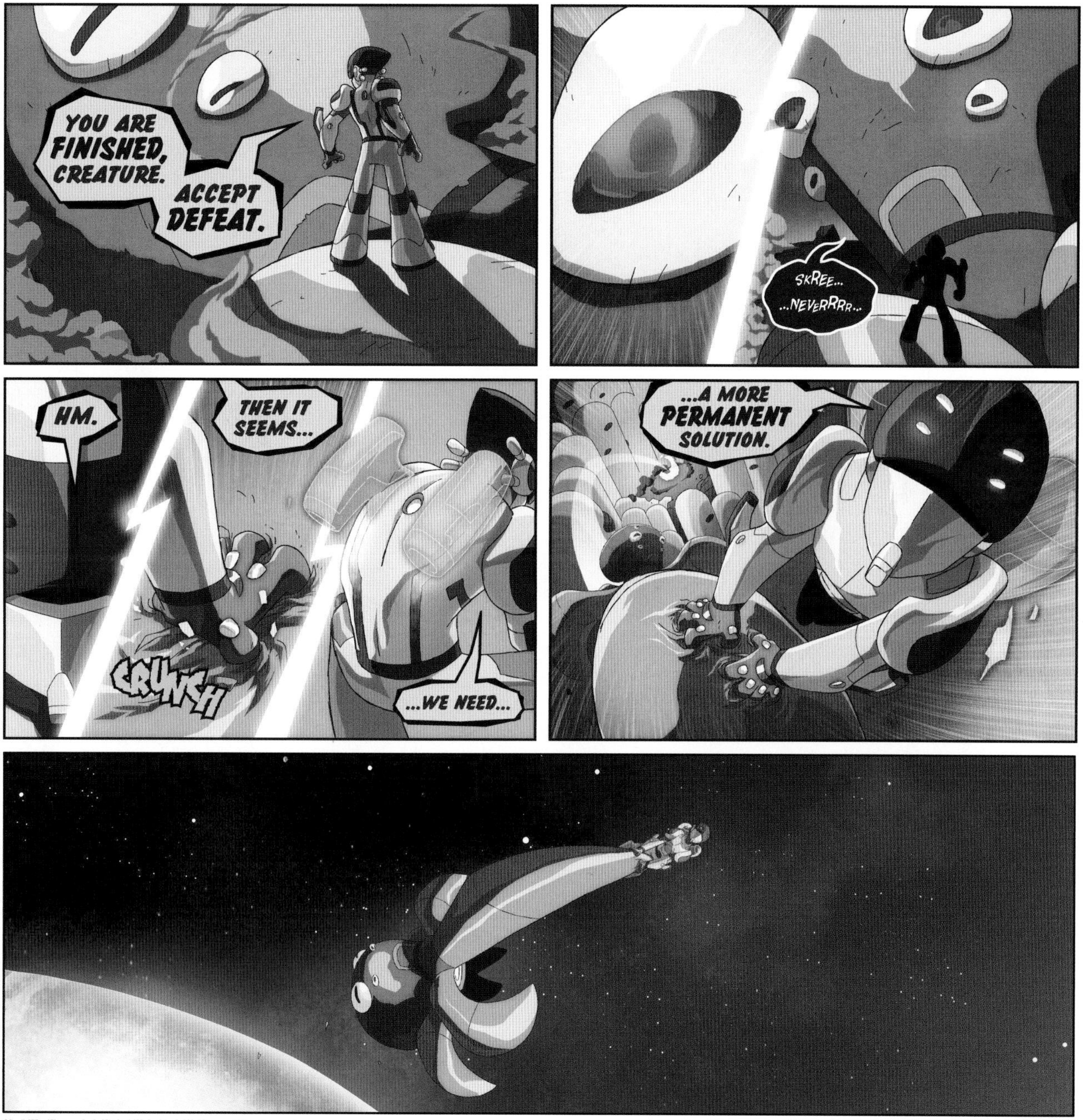
YOU ARE FINISHED, CREATURE.
ACCEPT DEFEAT.
SKREE... ...NEVERRRR...
HM.
THEN IT SEEMS...
CRUNCH
...WE NEED...
...A MORE PERMANENT SOLUTION.

#128: MANEUVER: ZULU

FEBRUARY 09, 2013

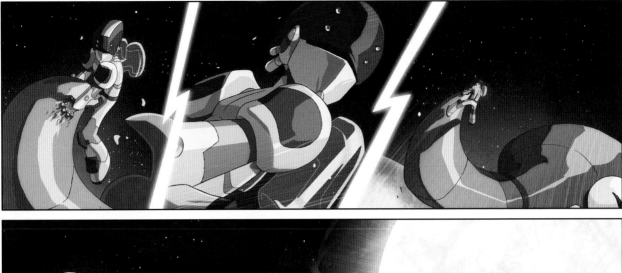

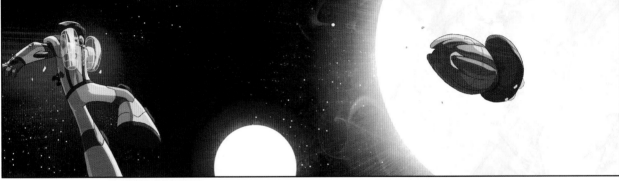

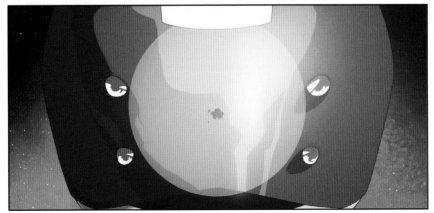

#129: FINAL MANEUVER

FEBRUARY 12, 2013

#130: BRAVILOGUE

FEBRUARY 14, 2013

COMMENTS

MATT: Farewell, Bravo Master! We hardly saw ye fling but one giant alien cyber-octopus into a star...

DAX: I liked Matt's idea to have the transformation or power-down sequence be comedic and clumsy. I feel that totally represents the *Bravoman* theme perfectly and was the right way to contradict the fairly serious action scene that just took place.

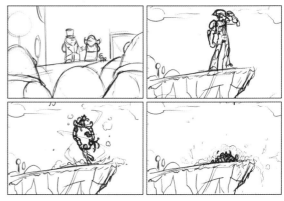

ROUGH LAYOUT

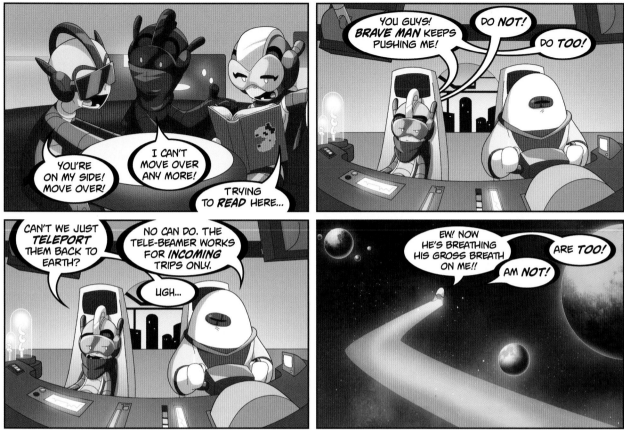

#131: BACK SEAT BRAVOS   FEBRUARY 16, 2013

COMMENTS

MATT: I think this one is a great example of the *flexible age* our characters' personalities have. I like to say that depending on the situation, Bravoman is age 15 to 35, and most of the rest of the characters follow suit.

DAX: A callback to Bravo Woman's X-mas gift, another cool Matt-ism.

FINAL WORDS

MATT: *Bravoman* has seriously been one of the funnest projects I have ever gotten to work on (I decree that *funnest* is an actual word, gosh durn it). I'm so glad it's now made it into print form. See you in Volume 2!

DAX: I have had a blast working on this series and I hope you have all enjoyed reading it just as much. I can't thank you enough for your continued support!!! 'Till next time! #BravoFansRule #BravoLove

DAX GORDINE
SKETCH GALLERY

BRAVOMAN
SUPER-UNEQUALED HERO OF EXCELLENCE

ALPHA MAN
ALIEN SIDEKICK OF
SUPREME MENTORING

LOTTERY MAN
SNACK-CONVEYING MOBILE ROBOT

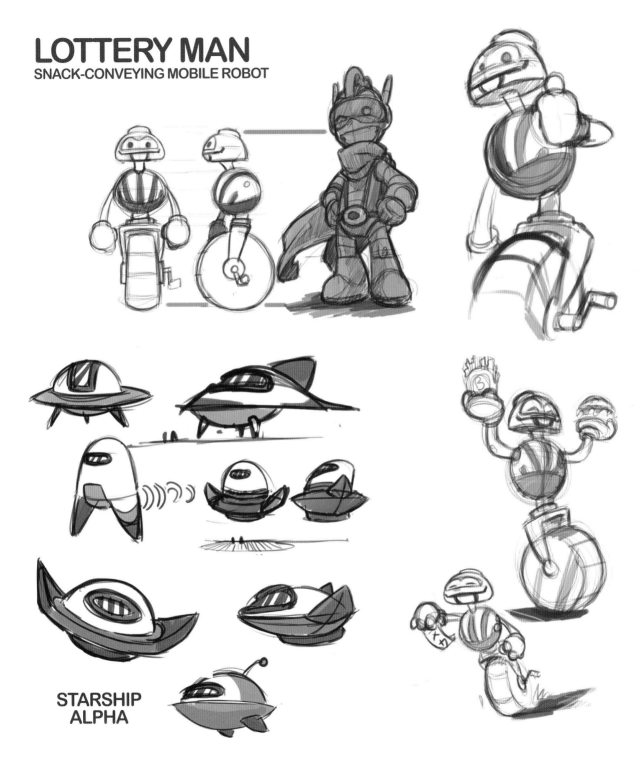

STARSHIP
ALPHA

WAYA HIME
NINJA PRINCESS WITH BLADED HEARTS

DR. BOMB
SCIENTIFIC VILLAIN OF
INCREDIBLE SPEECH

CAMO
INVISIBLE ARBORIST NINJA

PISTOL DAIMYO
HIGH-FLYING FEUDAL LORD

KOMUSO
MUSICAL BASKET NINJA

KARASU TENGU
HENCHLING CROW DEMON ARMY

WONDER
MOMO
TEEN BATTLE IDOL

ZULU
TENTACLE WARLORD OF SINISTER DOOM

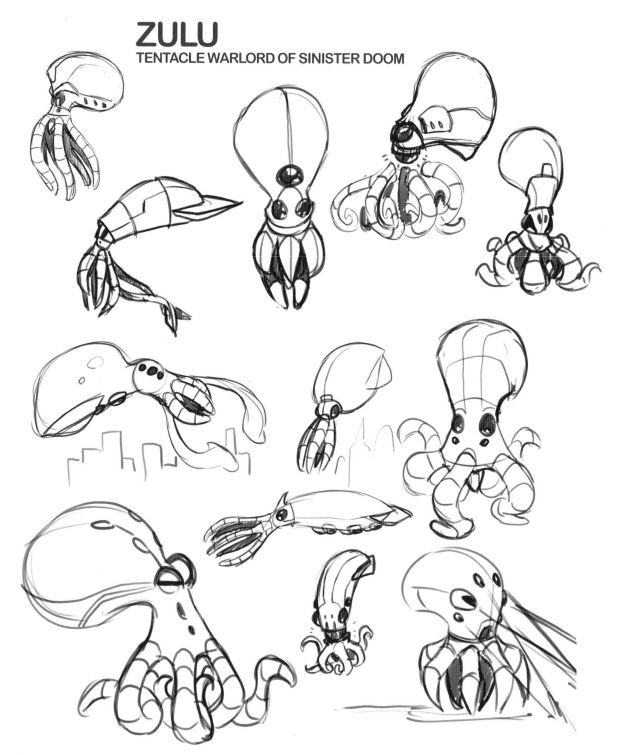

BRAVO MASTER
ULTIMATE FUSION OF RIGHTEOUS HEROISM

Bravoman Tribute Art.: JEFFREY "CHAMBA" CRUZ

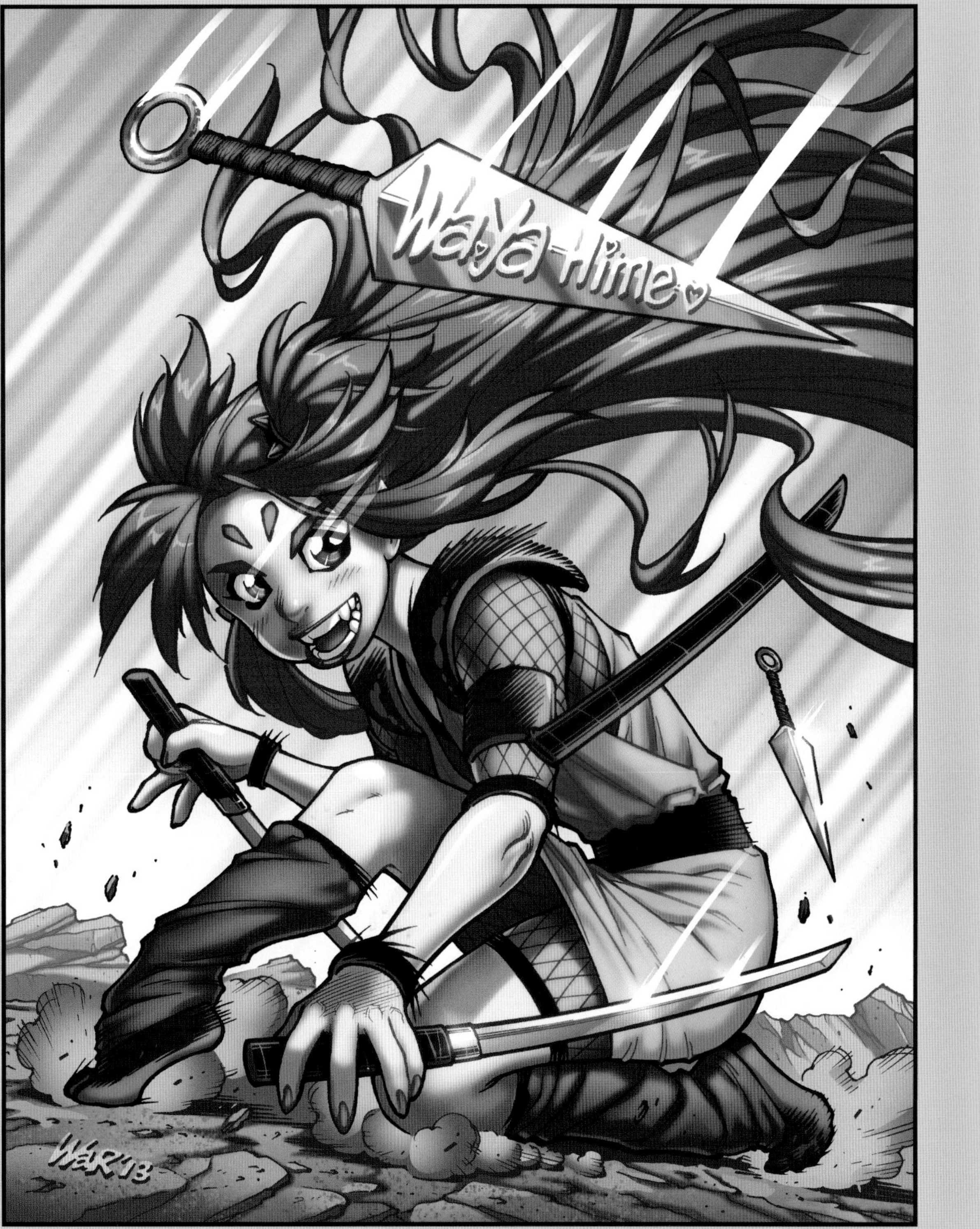
WaYa Hime
WaR'13

Bravoman Tribute Art : ADAM WARREN with ESPEN GRUNDETJERN

Bravoman Tribute Art : JOSH PEREZ

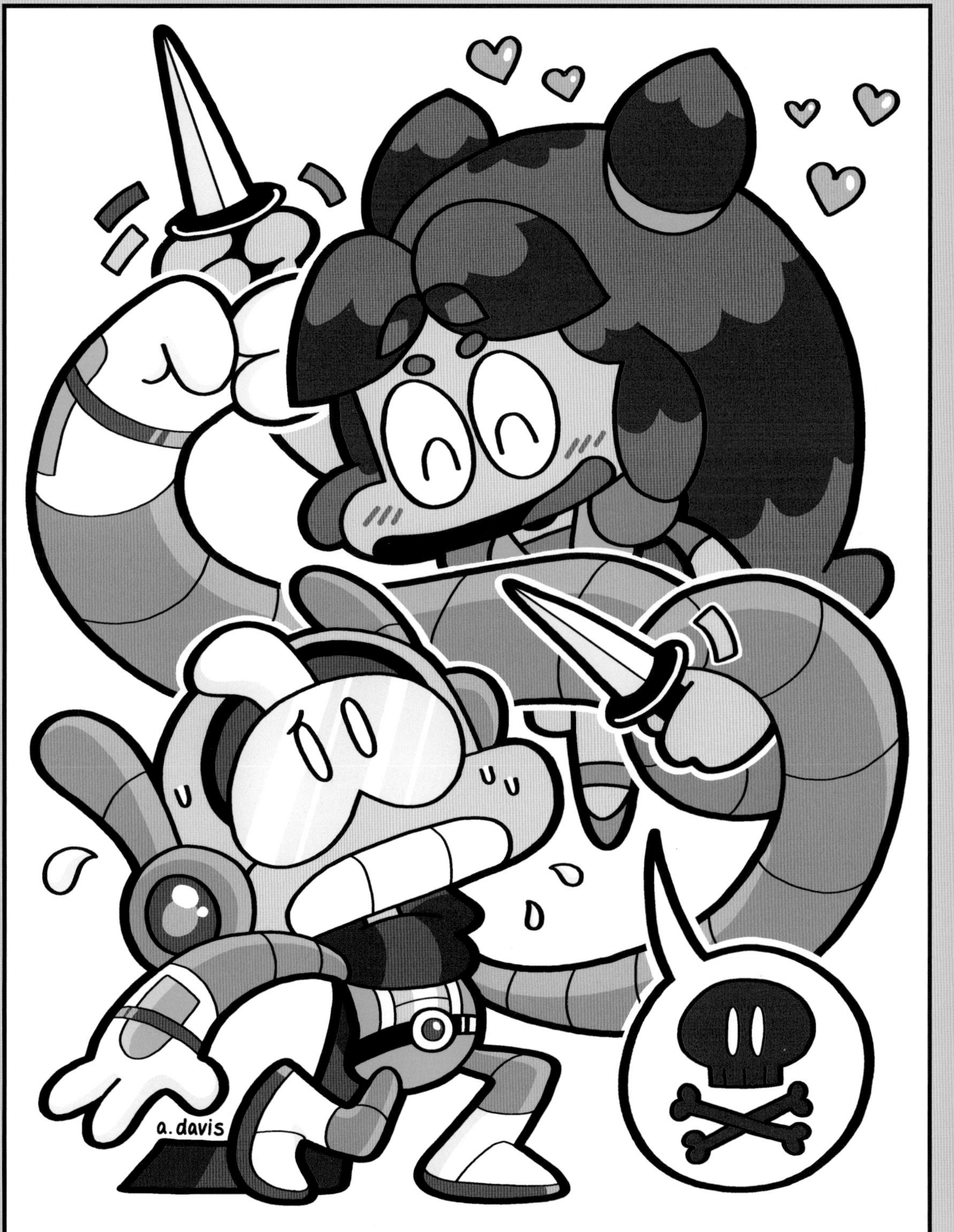
a.davis

Bravoman Tribute Art : ASHLEY DAVIS

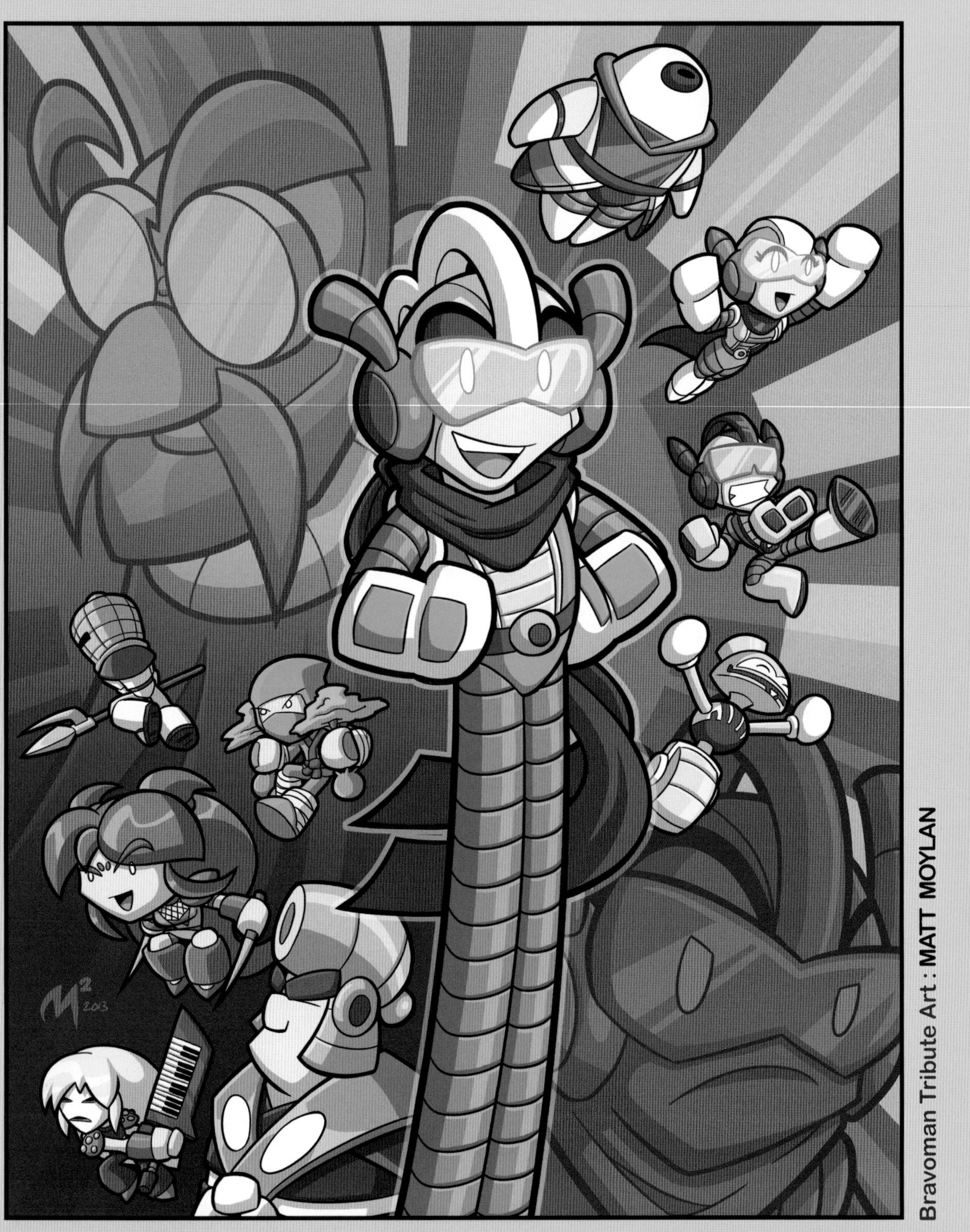

Bravoman Tribute Art : **MATT MOYLAN**

Bravoman Tribute Art : **SEAN GALLOWAY with TABLE TAFFY STUDIO**

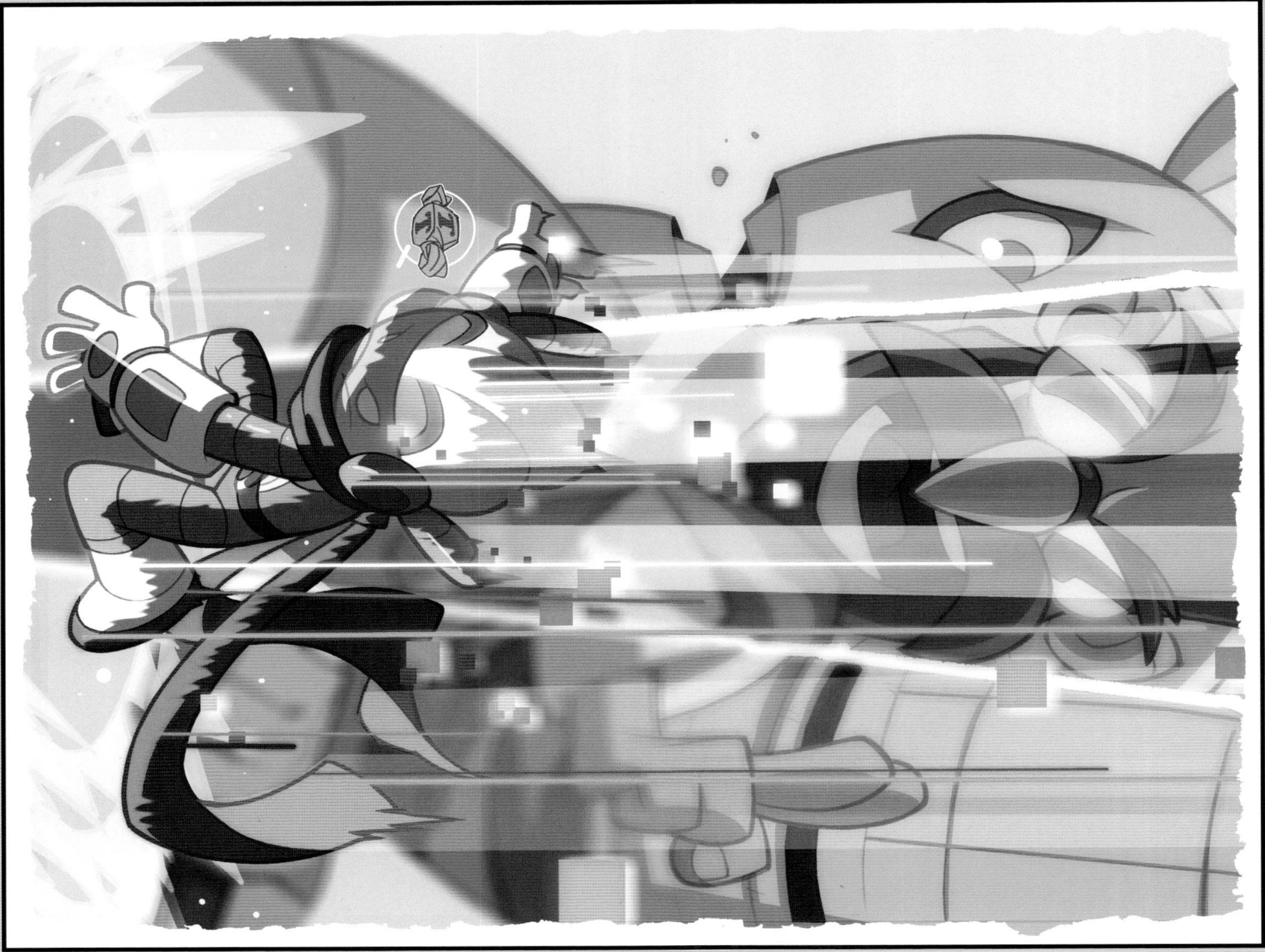

Bravoman Tribute Art : JAMES GHIO

Bravoman Tribute Art : HITOSHI ARIGA

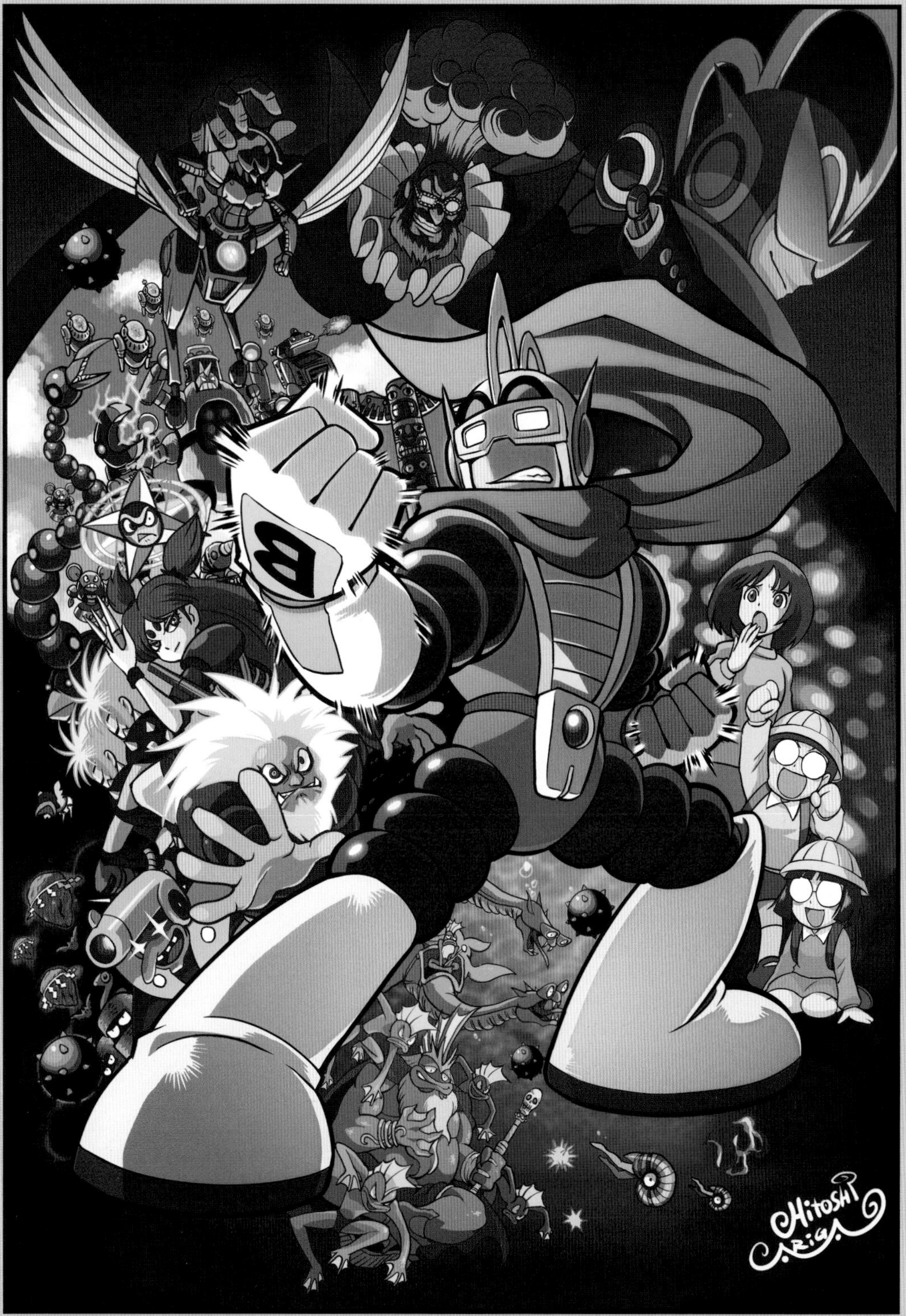
B
Hitoshi
Ariga

Bravoman Tribute Art : GONZALO ORDÓÑEZ ARIAS (GENZOMAN)

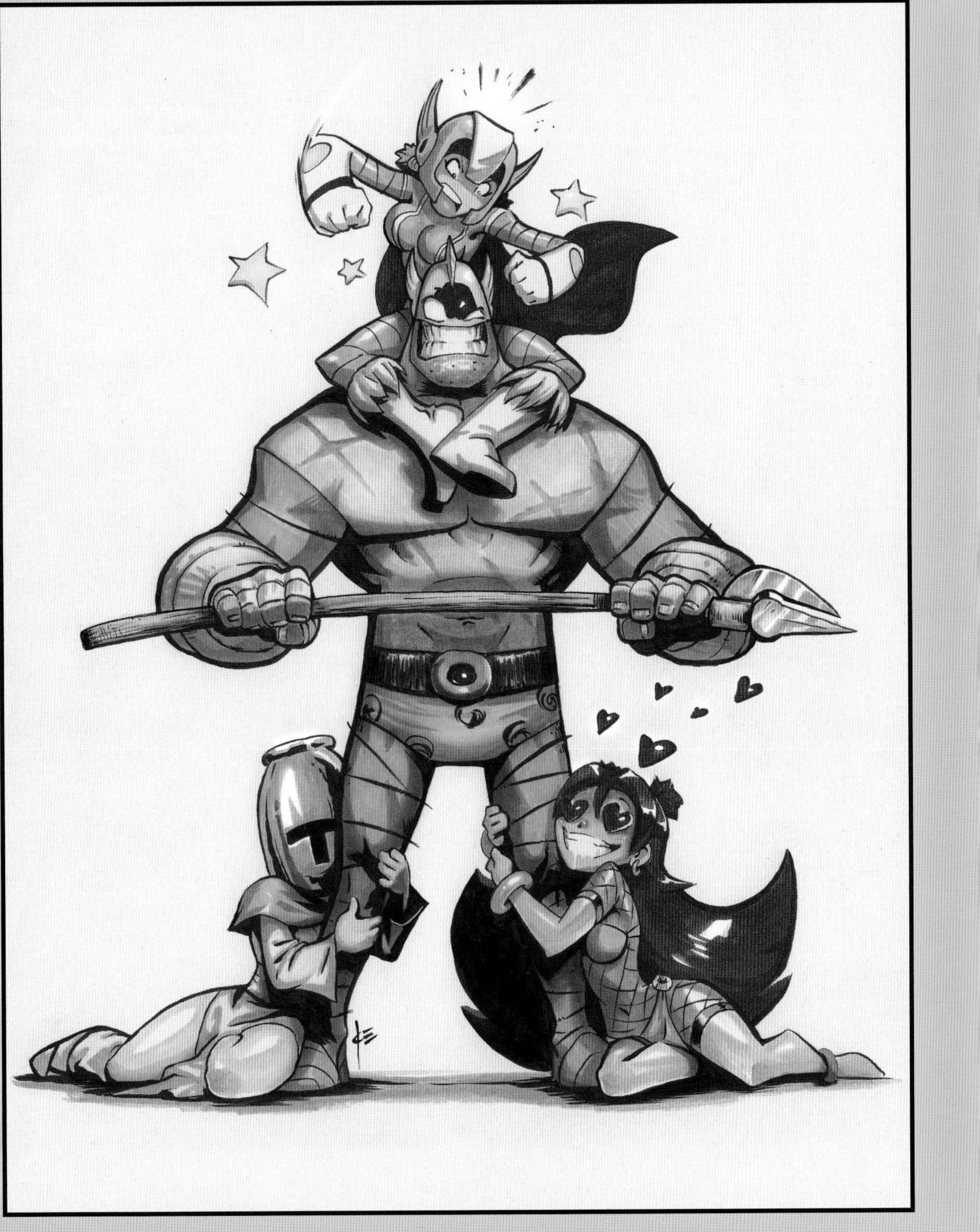

Bravoman Tribute Art : **JOE VRIENS**

Bravoman Tribute Art : DAX GORDINE with JOSH PEREZ

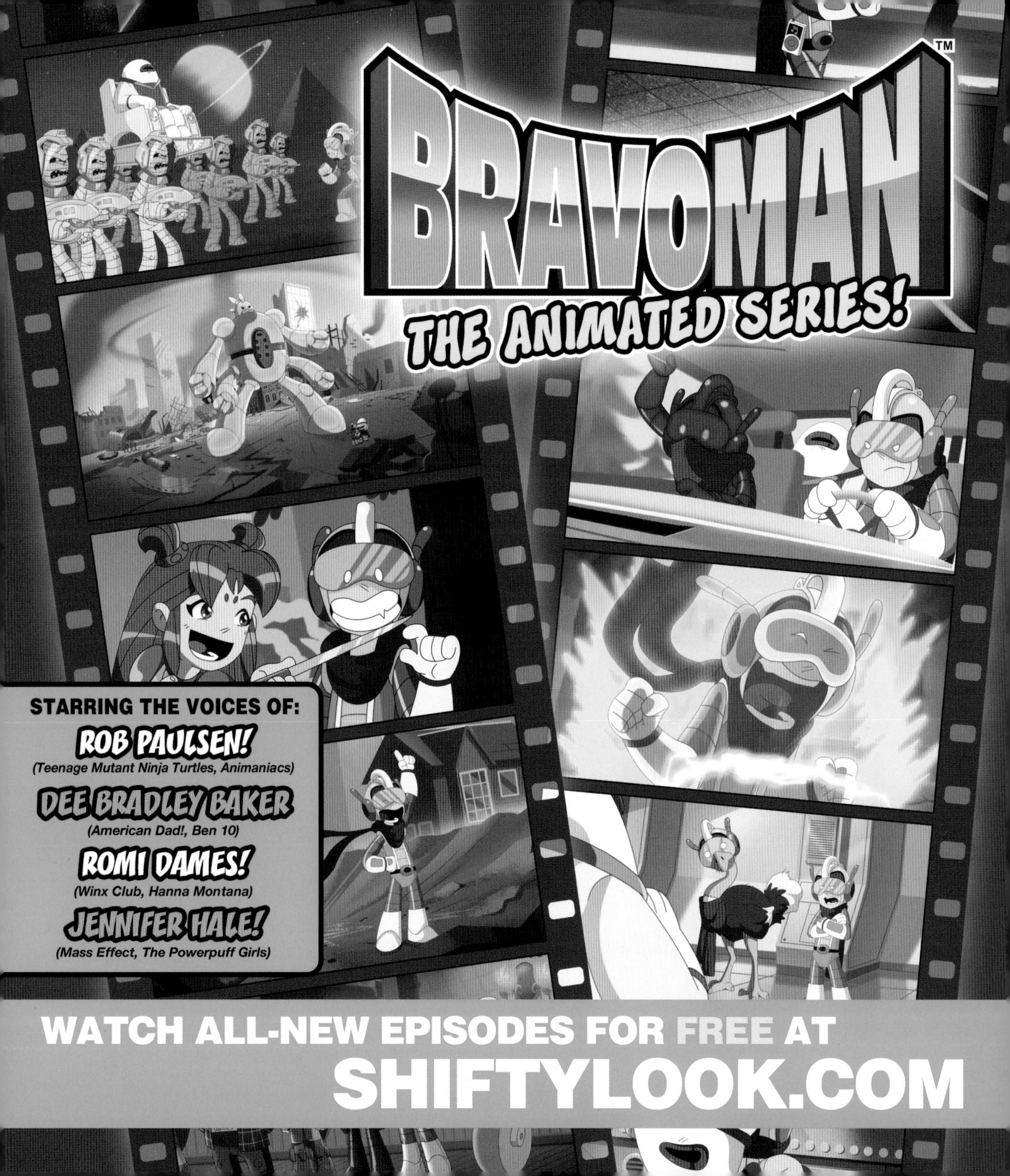
BRAVOMAN™
THE ANIMATED SERIES!
STARRING THE VOICES OF:
ROB PAULSEN!
(Teenage Mutant Ninja Turtles, Animaniacs)
DEE BRADLEY BAKER
(American Dad!, Ben 10)
ROMI DAMES!
(Winx Club, Hanna Montana)
JENNIFER HALE!
(Mass Effect, The Powerpuff Girls)
WATCH ALL-NEW EPISODES FOR FREE AT
SHIFTYLOOK.COM

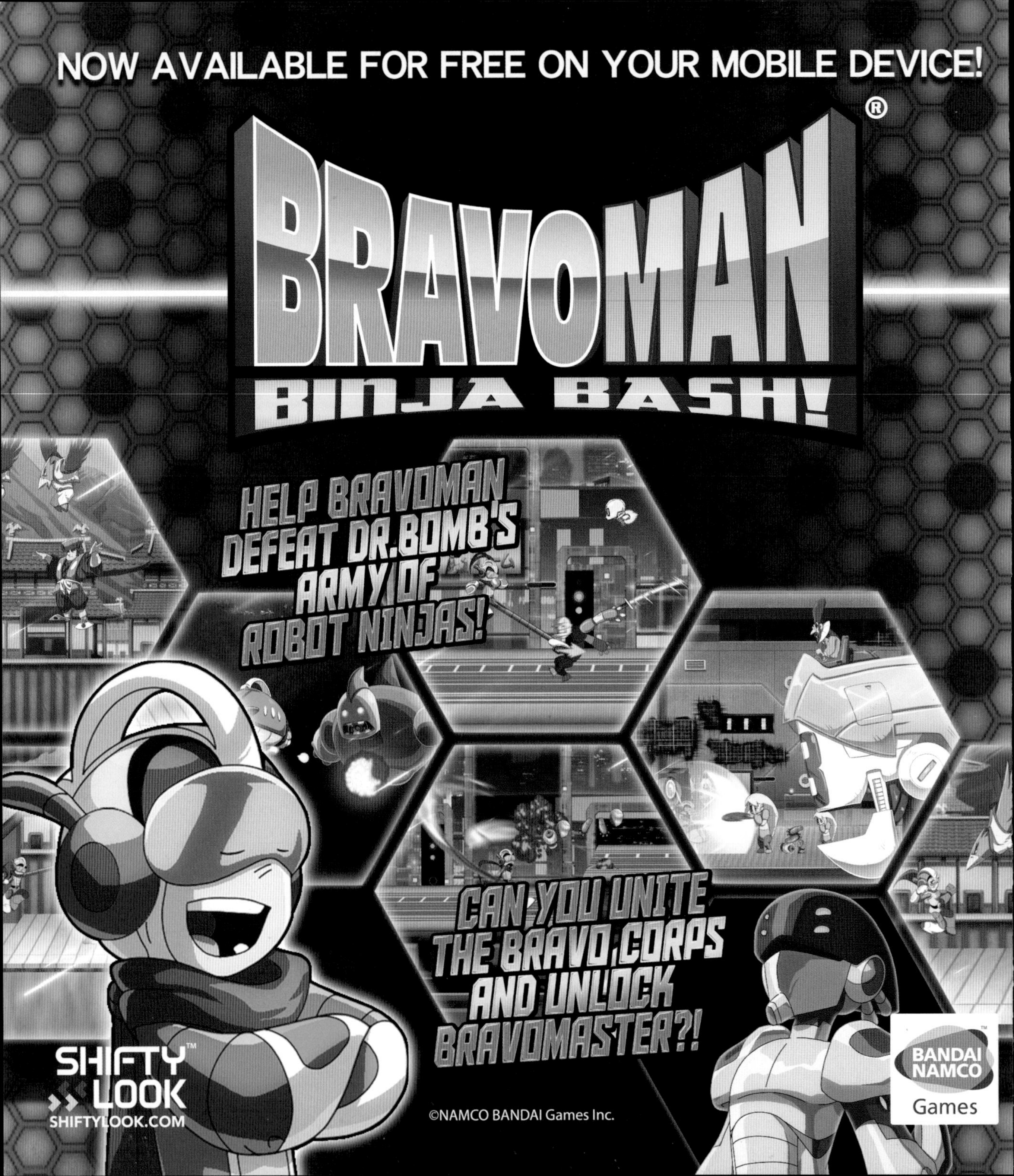
NOW AVAILABLE FOR FREE ON YOUR MOBILE DEVICE!
BRAVOMAN®
BINJA BASH!
HELP BRAVOMAN DEFEAT DR.BOMB'S ARMY OF ROBOT NINJAS!
CAN YOU UNITE THE BRAVO CORPS AND UNLOCK BRAVOMASTER?!
SHIFTY™ LOOK
SHIFTYLOOK.COM
©NAMCO BANDAI Games Inc.
BANDAI NAMCO Games

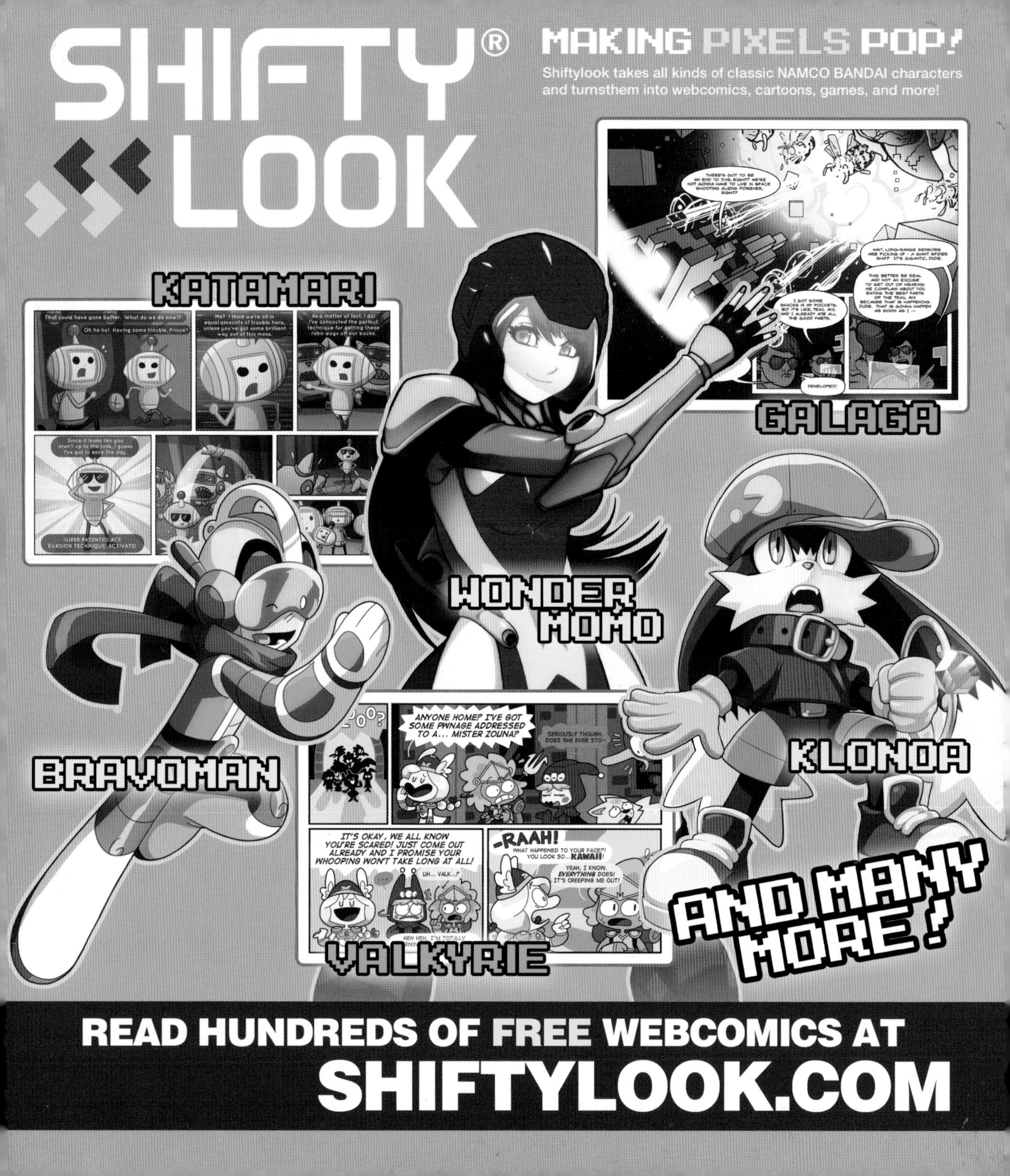
SHIFTY® LOOK
MAKING PIXELS POP!
Shiftylook takes all kinds of classic NAMCO BANDAI characters and turnsthem into webcomics, cartoons, games, and more!
THERE'S GOT TO BE AN END TO THIS, RIGHT? WE'RE NOT GONNA HAVE TO LIVE IN SPACE SHOOTING ALIENS FOREVER, RIGHT?
WAIT, LONG-RANGE SENSORS ARE PICKING UP - A GIANT SPIDER SHIP? IT'S GIGANTIC, DUDE.
THIS BETTER BE REAL AND NOT AN EXCUSE TO GET OUT OF HEARING ME COMPLAIN ABOUT YOU EATING THE BEST PARTS OF THE TRAIL MIX BECAUSE THAT IS HAPPENING DUDE. THAT IS GONNA HAPPEN AS SOON AS I --
I GOT SOME SNACKS IN MY POCKETS. BUT IT'S LIKE, TRAIL MIX. AND I ALREADY ATE ALL THE GOOD PARTS.
PENELOPE!!!
GALAGA
KATAMARI
That could have gone better. What do we do now?!
Oh ho ho! Having some trouble, Prince?
Me? I think we're all in equal amounts of trouble here, unless you've got some brilliant way out of this mess.
As a matter of fact, I do! I've concocted the perfect technique for getting these robo-dogs off our backs.
Since it looks like you aren't up to the task, I guess I've got to save the day.
SUPER PATENTED ACE EVASION TECHNIQUE: ACTIVATE!
WONDER MOMO
KLONOA
BRAVOMAN
ANYONE HOME? I'VE GOT SOME PWNAGE ADDRESSED TO A... MISTER ZOUNA?
SERIOUSLY THOUGH, DOES SHE EVER STO--
IT'S OKAY, WE ALL KNOW YOU'RE SCARED! JUST COME OUT ALREADY AND I PROMISE YOUR WHOOPING WON'T TAKE LONG AT ALL!
UH... VALK...?
-RAAH!
WHAT HAPPENED TO YOUR FACE?! YOU LOOK SO... KAWAII!
YEAH, I KNOW. EVERYTHING DOES! IT'S CREEPING ME OUT!
VALKYRIE
AND MANY MORE!
READ HUNDREDS OF FREE WEBCOMICS AT
SHIFTYLOOK.COM

BRAVOMAN
SUPER-UNEQUALED HERO OF EXCELLENCE!

MATT MOYLAN
(Writer, Lettering)

DAX "D-GEE" GORDINE
(Pencils, Inks, Colors)

JOSH PEREZ
(Colors)

Special Thanks:
JOE VRIENS - ROB PORTER (ROBAATO) - JEFFREY CRUZ (CHAMBA) - JAMES GHIO
EDWIN HUANG - ADAM WARREN - GONZALO ORDÓÑEZ ARIAS (GENZOMAN)
ASHLEY DAVIS - SEAN "CHEEKS" GALLOWAY (CHEEKS) - HITOSHI ARIGA

UDON ENTERTAINMENT

Chief of Operations - ERIK KO
Managing Editor - MATT MOYLAN
Project Manager - JIM ZUBKAVICH
Director of Marketing - CHRISTOPHER BUTCHER
Marketing Manager - STACY KING
Associate Editor - ASH PAULSEN
Japanese Liaisons - M. KIRIE HAYASHI
                   STEVEN CUMMINGS

SHIFTYLOOK (NAMCO BANDAI Games Inc.)

Managing Director,
Head of Production Group 1, NBGI - MAKOTO ASANUMA

Executive Producer, ShiftyLook - YUTARO IKEGAYA

Producer & Editor-in-Chief, ShiftyLook - ROB PEREYDA

Team Shifty - CORY CASONI
             ASH PAULSEN
             THE NSO

BRAVOMAN VOLUME 1
© NAMCO BANDAI Games Inc.

Published by UDON Entertainment Corp.
118 Tower Hill Road, C1, PO Box 20008, Richmond Hill, Ontario, L4K 0K0, Canada

www.UDONentertainment.com

First Printing: November 2013
ISBN-13: 978-1-926778-93-8
ISBN-10 : 1-926778-93-6

Printed in China